...dington, Middlesex. He made ... *Vortex* (1924), in which he also ap... ...uccessful plays included *Fallen Angels* (192█/█ ... ...te Lives* (1933), *Design for Living* (1933), and *Blithe Spirit* (1941). ...ng the war he wrote screenplays such as *Brief Encounter* (1944) and *This Happy Breed* (1942). In the fifties he began a new career as a cabaret entertainer. He published volumes of verse and a novel (*Pomp and Circumstance*, 1960), two volumes of auto-biography and four volumes of short stories: *To Step Aside* (1939), *Star Quality* (1951), *Pretty Polly Barlow* (1964) and *Bon Voyage* (1967). He was knighted in 1970 and died three years later in Jamaica.

also by Nöel Coward

Coward
Collected Plays: One
(Hay Fever, The Vortex, Fallen Angels, Easy Virtue)

Collected Plays: Two
(Private Lives, Bitter-Sweet, The Marquise, Post-Mortem)

Collected Plays: Three
(Design for Living, Cavalcade, Conversation Piece,
and Hands Across the Sea, Still Life, Fumed Oak
from Tonight at 8.30)

Collected Plays: Four
(Blithe Spirit, Present Laughter, This Happy Breed,
and Ways and Means, The Astonished Heart, 'Red Peppers'
from Tonight at 8.30)

Collected Plays: Five
(Relative Values, Look After Lulu!,
Waiting in the Wings, Suite in Three Keys)

Collected Plays: Six
(Semi-Monde, Point Valaine, South Sea Bubble,
Nude With Violin)

Collected Plays: Seven
(Quadrille, 'Peace in Our Time',
and We Were Dancing, Shadow Play, Family Album, Star Chamber
from Tonight at 8.30)

Collected Plays: Eight
(I'll Leave it to You, The Young Idea, This Was a Man)

Collected Revue Sketches and Parodies

The Complete Lyrics of Nöel Coward

Collected Short Stories

Pomp and Circumstance
A Novel

Autobiography

Private Lives

Nöel Coward

methuen | drama

LONDON • NEW YORK • OXFORD • NEW DELHI • SYDNEY

METHUEN DRAMA
Bloomsbury Publishing Plc
50 Bedford Square, London, WC1B 3DP, UK
1385 Broadway, New York, NY 10018, USA

BLOOMSBURY, METHUEN DRAMA and the Methuen Drama logo are
trademarks of Bloomsbury Publishing Plc

First published 1930 by Heinemann and republished in 1934 in *Play Parade* Vol. I.
Published in *Noël Coward Plays: Two* by Eyre Methuen Ltd in 1979

This single-volume edition published in 2000 by Methuen Publishing Ltd

Reprinted 2018, 2019

A catalogue record for this book is available from the British Library.

A catalog record for this book is available from the Library of Congress.

ISBN: PB: 978-0-4137-4490-6
ePDF: 978-1-4725-0337-4
ePUB: 978-1-4081-7802-7

Series: Modern Classics

Printed and bound in Great Britain

To find out more about our authors and books visit
www.bloomsbury.com and sign up for our newsletters.

Private Lives

First produced at the Phoenix Theatre, London (after a preliminary tour), on 24 September 1930 with the following cast:

Amanda Prynne	Gertrude Lawrence
Victor Prynne, *her husband*	Laurence Olivier
Louise, *a maid*	Everly Craig
Sibyl Chase	Adrianne Allen
Elyot Chase, *her husband*	Noël Coward

Directed by Noël Coward
Designed by G. E. Calthrop

Act One
The terrace of a hotel in France. Summer evening.

Act Two
Amanda's flat in Paris. A few days later. Evening.

Act Three
The same. The next morning.

Time: The present.

Act One

The scene is the terrace of a hotel in France. There are two French windows at the back opening on to two separate suites. The terrace space is divided by a line of small trees in tubs, and, down-stage, running parallel with the footlights, there is a low stone balustrade. Upon each side of the line of tree tubs is a set of suitable terrace furniture, a swinging seat, two or three chairs, and a table. There are orange and white awnings shading the windows, as it is summer.

When the curtain rises it is about eight o'clock in the evening. There is an orchestra playing not very far off. **Sibyl Chase** *opens the windows on the right, and steps out on to the terrace. She is very pretty and blonde, and smartly dressed in travelling clothes. She comes down-stage, stretches her arms wide with a little sigh of satisfaction, and regards the view with an ecstatic expression.*

Sibyl (*calling*)   Elli, Elli dear, do come out. It's so lovely.

Elyot (*inside*)   Just a minute.

After a pause **Elyot** *comes out. He is about thirty, quite slim and pleasant looking, and also in travelling clothes. He walks right down to the balustrade and looks thoughtfully at the view.* **Sibyl** *stands beside him, and slips her arm through his.*

Elyot   Not so bad.

Sibyl   It's heavenly. Look at the lights of that yacht reflected in the water. Oh dear, I'm so happy.

Elyot (*smiling*)   Are you?

Sibyl   Aren't you?

Elyot   Of course I am. Tremendously happy.

Sibyl   Just to think, here we are, you and I, married!

Elyot   Yes, things have come to a pretty pass.

Sibyl   Don't laugh at me, you mustn't be *blasé* about honeymoons just because this is your second.

Elyot (*frowning*)   That's silly.

Sibyl   Have I annoyed you by saying that?

Elyot   Just a little.

Sibyl   Oh, darling, I'm so sorry. (*She holds her face up to his.*) Kiss me.

Elyot (*doing so*)   There.

Sibyl   Ummm, not so very enthusiastic.

Elyot (*kissing her again*)   That better?

Sibyl   Three times, please, I'm superstitious.

Elyot (*kissing her*)   You really are very sweet.

Sibyl   Are you glad you married me?

Elyot   Of course I am.

Sibyl   How glad?

Elyot   Incredibly, magnificently glad.

Sibyl   How lovely.

Elyot   We ought to go in and dress.

Sibyl   Gladder than before?

Elyot   Why do you keep harping on that?

Sibyl   It's in my mind, and yours too, I expect.

Sibyl   It isn't anything of the sort.

Sibyl   She was pretty, wasn't she? Amanda?

Elyot   Very pretty.

Sibyl   Prettier than I am?

Elyot   Much.

Sibyl   Elyot!

Elyot   She was pretty and sleek, and her hands were long and slim, and her legs were long and slim, and she danced like an angel. You dance very poorly, by the way.

Sibyl   Could she play the piano as well as I can?

Elyot   She couldn't play the piano at all.

Sibyl (*triumphantly*)   Aha! Had she my talent for organisation?

Elyot   No, but she hadn't your mother either.

Sibyl   I don't believe you like mother.

Elyot   Like her! I can't bear her.

Sibyl   Elyot! She's a darling, underneath.

Elyot   I never got underneath.

Sibyl   It makes me unhappy to think you don't like mother.

Elyot   Nonsense. I believe the only reason you married me was to get away from her.

Sibyl   I married you because I loved you.

Elyot   Oh dear, oh dear, oh dear, oh dear!

Elyot   I love you far more than Amanda loved you. I'd never make you miserable like she did.

Elyot   We made each other miserable.

Sibyl   It was all her fault, you know it was.

Elyot (*with vehemence*)   Yes, it was. Entirely her fault.

Sibyl   She was a fool to lose you.

Elyot   We lost each other.

Sibyl   She lost you, with her violent tempers and carryings-on.

Elyot   Will you stop talking about Amanda?

Sibyl   But I'm very glad, because if she hadn't been uncontrolled, and wicked, and unfaithful, we shouldn't be here now.

Elyot She wasn't unfaithful.

Sibyl How do you know? I bet she was. I bet she was unfaithful every five minutes.

Elyot It would take a far more concentrated woman than Amanda to be unfaithful every five minutes.

Sibyl (*anxiously*) You do hate her, don't you?

Elyot No, I don't hate her. I think I despise her.

Sibyl (*with satisfaction*) That's much worse.

Elyot And yet I'm sorry for her.

Sibyl Why?

Elyot Because she's marked for tragedy; she's bound to make a mess of everything.

Sibyl If it's all her fault, I don't see that it matters much.

Elyot She has some very good qualities.

Sibyl Considering what a hell she made of your life, I think you are very nice about her. Most men would be vindictive.

Elyot What's the use of that? It's all over now, such a long time ago.

Sibyl Five years isn't very long.

Elyot (*seriously*) Yes it is.

Sibyl Do you think you could ever love her again?

Elyot Now then, Sibyl.

Sibyl But could you?

Elyot Of course not, I love you.

Sibyl Yes, but you love me differently; I know that.

Elyot More wisely perhaps.

Sibyl I'm glad. I'd rather have that sort of love.

Elyot You're right. Love is no use unless it's wise, and kind, and undramatic. Something steady and sweet, to smooth out your nerves when you're tired. Something tremendously cosy; and unflurried by scenes and jealousies. That's what I want, what I've always wanted really. Oh my dear, I do hope it's not going to be dull for you.

Sibyl Sweetheart, as tho' you could ever be dull.

Elyot I'm much older than you.

Sibyl Not so very much.

Elyot Seven years.

Sibyl (*snuggling up to him*) The music has stopped now and you can hear the sea.

Elyot We'll bathe to-morrow morning.

Sibyl I mustn't get sunburnt.

Elyot Why not?

Sibyl I hate it on women.

Elyot Very well, you shan't then. I hope you don't hate it on men.

Sibyl Of course I don't. It's suitable to men.

Elyot You're a completely feminine little creature, aren't you?

Sibyl Why do you say that?

Elyot Everything in its place.

Sibyl What do you mean?

Elyot If you feel you'd like me to smoke a pipe, I'll try and master it.

Sibyl I like a man to be a man, if that's what you mean.

Elyot Are you going to understand me, and manage me?

Sibyl I'm going to try to understand you.

Elyot Run me without my knowing it?

Sibyl (*withdrawing slightly*)   I think you're being a little unkind.

Elyot   No, I don't mean to be. I was only wondering.

Sibyl   Well?

Elyot   I was wondering what was going on inside your mind, what your plans are really?

Sibyl   Plans; Oh, Elli!

Elyot   Apart from loving me and all that, you must have plans.

Sibyl   I haven't the faintest idea what you're talking about.

Elyot   Perhaps it's subconscious then, age-old instincts working away deep down, mincing up little bits of experience for future use, watching me carefully like a little sharp-eyed, blonde kitten.

Sibyl   How can you be so horrid.

Elyot   I said Kitten, not Cat.

Sibyl   Kittens grow into cats.

Elyot   Let that be a warning to you.

Sibyl (*slipping her arm through his again*)   What's the matter, darling; are you hungry?

Elyot   Not a bit.

Sibyl   You're very strange all of a sudden, and rather cruel. Just because I'm feminine. It doesn't mean that I'm crafty and calculating.

Elyot   I didn't say you were either of those things.

Sibyl   I hate these half masculine women who go banging about.

Elyot   I hate anybody who goes banging about.

Sibyl   I should think you needed a little quiet womanliness after Amanda.

Elyot   Why will you keep on talking about her?

Sibyl It's natural enough, isn't it?

Elyot What do you want to find out?

Sibyl Why did you really let her divorce you?

Elyot She divorced me for cruelty, and flagrant infidelity. I spent a whole week-end at Brighton with a lady called Vera Williams. She had the nastiest looking hair brush I have ever seen.

Sibyl Misplaced chivalry, I call it. Why didn't you divorce her?

Elyot It would not have been the action of a gentleman, whatever that may mean.

Sibyl I think she got off very lightly.

Elyot Once and for all will you stop talking about her.

Sibyl Yes, Elli dear.

Elyot I don't wish to see her again or hear her name mentioned.

Sibyl Very well, darling.

Elyot Is that understood?

Sibyl Yes, darling. Where did you spend your honeymoon?

Elyot St Moritz. Be quiet.

Sibyl I hate St Moritz.

Elyot So do I, bitterly.

Sibyl Was she good on skis?

Elyot Do you want to dine downstairs here, or at the Casino?

Sibyl I love you, I love you, I love you.

Elyot Good, let's go in and dress.

Sibyl Kiss me first.

Elyot (*kissing her*) Casino?

Sibyl   Yes. Are you a gambler? You never told me.

Elyot   Every now and then.

Sibyl   I shall come and sit just behind your chair and bring you luck.

Elyot   That will be fatal.

*They go off into their suite. There is a slight pause and then **Victor Prynne** enters from the left suite. He is quite nice looking, about thirty or thirty-five. He is dressed in a light travelling suit. He sniffs the air, looks at the view, and then turns back to the window.*

Victor (*calling*)   Mandy.

Amanda (*inside*)   What?

Victor   Come outside, the view is wonderful.

Amanda   I'm still damp from the bath. Wait a minute –

Victor *lights a cigarette. Presently **Amanda** comes out on to the terrace. She is quite exquisite with a gay face and a perfect figure. At the moment she is wearing a negligee.*

Amanda   I shall catch pneumonia, that's what I shall catch.

Victor (*looking at her*)   God!

Amanda   I beg your pardon?

Victor   You look wonderful.

Amanda   Thank you, darling.

Victor   Like a beautiful advertisement for something.

Amanda   Nothing peculiar, I hope.

Victor   I can hardly believe it's true. You and I, here alone together, married!

Amanda (*rubbing her face on his shoulder*)   That stuff's very rough.

Victor   Don't you like it?

Amanda   A bit hearty, isn't it?

Victor   Do you love me?

Amanda   Of course, that's why I'm here.

Victor   More than –

Amanda   Now then, none of that.

Victor   No, but do you love me more than you loved Elyot?

Amanda   I don't remember, it's such a long time ago.

Victor   Not so very long.

Amanda (*flinging out her arms*)   All my life ago.

Victor   I'd like to break his damned neck.

Amanda (*laughing*)   Why?

Victor   For making you so unhappy.

Amanda   It was mutual.

Victor   Rubbish! It was all his fault, you know it was.

Amanda   Yes, it was, now I come to think about it.

Victor   Swine!

Amanda   Don't be so vehement, darling.

Victor   I'll never treat you like that.

Amanda   That's right.

Victor   I love you too much.

Amanda   So did he.

Victor   Fine sort of love that is. He struck you once, didn't he?

Amanda   More than once.

Victor   Where?

Amanda   Several places.

Victor   What a cad.

Amanda   I struck him too. Once I broke four gramophone records over his head. It was very satisfying.

Victor   You must have been driven to distraction.

Amanda   Yes, I was, but don't let's talk about it, please. After all, it's a dreary subject for our honeymoon night.

Victor   He didn't know when he was well off.

Amanda   Look at the lights of that yacht reflected in the water. I wonder whose it is.

Victor   We must bathe to-morrow.

Amanda   Yes. I want to get a nice sunburn.

Victor (*reproachfully*)   Mandy!

Amanda   Why, what's the matter?

Victor   I hate sunburnt women.

Amanda   Why?

Victor   It's somehow, well, unsuitable.

Amanda   It's awfully suitable to me, darling.

Victor   Of course if you really want to.

Amanda   I'm absolutely determined. I've got masses of lovely oil to rub all over myself.

Victor   Your skin is so beautiful as it is.

Amanda   Wait and see. When I'm done a nice crisp brown, you'll fall in love with me all over again.

Victor   I couldn't love you move than I do now.

Amanda   Oh, dear. I did so hope our honeymoon was going to be progressive.

Victor   Where did you spend the last one?

Amanda (*warningly*)   Victor.

Victor   I want to know.

Amanda   St Moritz. It was very attractive.

Victor   I hate St Moritz.

Amanda   So do I.

Victor   Did he start quarrelling with you right away?

Amanda   Within the first few days. I put it down to the high altitudes.

Victor   And you loved him?

Amanda   Yes, Victor.

Victor   You poor child.

Amanda   You must try not to be pompous, dear. (*She turns away.*)

Victor (*hurt*)   Mandy!

Amanda   I don't believe I'm a bit like what you think I am.

Victor   How do you mean?

Amanda   I was never a poor child.

Victor   Figure of speech, dear, that's all.

Amanda   I suffered a great deal, and had my heart broken. But it wasn't an innocent girlish heart. It was jagged with sophistication. I've always been sophisticated, far too knowing. That caused many of my rows with Elyot. I irritated him because he knew I could see through him.

Victor   I don't mind how much you see through me.

Amanda   Sweet. (*She kisses him.*)

Victor   I'm going to make you happy.

Amanda   Are you?

Victor   Just by looking after you, and seeing that you're all right, you know.

Amanda (*a trifle wistfully*)   No, I don't know.

Victor   I think you love me quite differently from the way you loved Elyot.

Amanda   Do stop harping on Elyot.

Victor   It's true, though, isn't it?

Amanda   I love you much more calmly, if that's what you mean.

Victor   More lastingly?

Amanda   I expect so.

Victor   Do you remember when I first met you?

Amanda   Yes. Distinctly.

Victor   At Marion Vale's party.

Amanda   Yes.

Victor   Wasn't it wonderful?

Amanda   Not really, dear. It was only redeemed from the completely commonplace by the fact of my having hiccoughs.

Victor   I never noticed them.

Amanda   Love at first sight.

Victor   Where did you first meet Elyot?

Amanda   To hell with Elyot.

Victor   Mandy!

Amanda   I forbid you to mention his name again. I'm sick of the sound of it. You must be raving mad. Here we are on the first night of our honeymoon, with the moon coming up, and the music playing, and all you can do is talk about my first husband. It's downright sacrilegious.

Victor   Don't be angry.

Amanda   Well, it's very annoying.

Victor   Will you forgive me?

Amanda   Yes; only don't do it again.

Victor   I promise.

Amanda   You'd better go and dress now, you haven't bathed yet.

Victor   Where shall we dine, downstairs here, or at the Casino?

Amanda   The Casino is more fun, I think.

Victor   We can play Boule afterwards.

Amanda   No, we can't, dear.

Victor   Don't you like dear old Boule?

Amanda   No, I hate dear old Boule. We'll play a nice game of Chemin de fer.

Victor (*apprehensively*)   Not at the big table?

Amanda   Maybe at the biggest table.

Victor   You're not a terrible gambler, are you?

Amanda   Inveterate. Chance rules my life.

Victor   What nonsense.

Amanda   How can you say it's nonsense. It was chance meeting you. It was chancing falling in love; it's chance that we're here, particularly after your driving. Everything that happens is chance.

Victor   You know I feel rather scared of you at close quarters.

Amanda   That promises to be very embarrassing.

Victor   You're somehow different now, wilder than I thought you were, more strained.

Amanda   Wilder! Oh Victor, I've never felt less wild in my life. A little strained, I grant you, but that's the newly married atmosphere; you can't expect anything else. Honeymooning is a very overrated amusement.

Victor   You say that because you had a ghastly experience before.

Amanda   There you go again.

Victor   It couldn't fail to embitter you a little.

Amanda   The honeymoon wasn't such a ghastly experience really; it was afterwards that was so awful.

Victor   I intend to make you forget it all entirely.

Amanda   You won't succeed by making constant references to it.

Victor   I wish I knew you better.

Amanda   It's just as well you don't. The 'woman' – in italics – should always retain a certain amount of alluring feminine mystery for the 'man' – also in italics.

Victor   What about the man? Isn't he allowed to have any mystery?

Amanda   Absolutely none. Transparent as glass.

Victor   Oh, I see.

Amanda   Never mind, darling; it doesn't necessarily work out like that; it's only supposed to.

Victor   I'm glad I'm normal.

Amanda   What an odd thing to be glad about. Why?

Victor   Well, aren't you?

Amanda   I'm not so sure I'm normal.

Victor   Oh, Mandy, of course you are, sweetly, divinely normal.

Amanda   I haven't any peculiar cravings for Chinamen or old boots, if that's what you mean.

Victor (*scandalised*)   Mandy!

Amanda   I think very few people are completely normal really, deep down in their private lives. It all depends on a combination of circumstances. If all the various cosmic thingummies fuse at the same moment, and the right spark is struck, there's no knowing what one mightn't do. That was the trouble with Elyot and me, we were like two violent acids bubbling about in a nasty little matrimonial bottle.

Victor   I don't believe you're nearly as complex as you think you are.

Amanda   I don't think I'm particularly complex, but I know I'm unreliable.

Victor   You're frightening me horribly. In what way unreliable?

Amanda   I'm so apt to see things the wrong way round.

Victor   What sort of things?

Amanda   Morals. What one should do and what one shouldn't.

Victor (*fondly*)   Darling, you're so sweet.

Amanda   Thank you, Victor, that's most encouraging. You really must have your bath now. Come along.

Victor   Kiss me.

Amanda (*doing so*)   There, dear, hurry now; I've only got to slip my dress on and then I shall be ready.

Victor   Give me ten minutes.

Amanda   I'll bring the cocktails out here when they come.

Victor   All right.

Amanda   Go along now, hurry.

They both disappear into their suite. After a moment's pause **Elyot** *steps carefully on to the terrace carrying a tray upon which are two champagne cocktails. He puts the tray down on the table.*

Elyot (*calling*)   Sibyl.

Sibyl (*inside*)   Yes.

Elyot   I've brought the cocktails out here, hurry up.

Sibyl   I can't find my lipstick.

Elyot   Never mind, send down to the kitchen for some cochineal.

Sibyl   Don't be so silly.

Elyot   Hurry.

Elyot saunters down to the balustrade. He looks casually over on to the next terrace, and then out at the view. He looks up at the moon and sighs, then he sits down in a chair with his back towards the line of tubs, and lights a cigarette. **Amanda** *steps gingerly on to her terrace carrying a tray with two champagne cocktails on it. She is wearing a charmingly simple evening gown, her cloak is flung over her right shoulder. She places the tray carefully on the table, puts her cloak over the back of a chair, and sits down with her back towards* **Elyot**. *She takes a small mirror from her handbag, and scrutinises her face in it. The orchestra downstairs strikes up a new melody. Both* **Elyot** *and* **Amanda** *give a little start. After a moment,* **Elyot** *pensively begins to hum the tune the band is playing. It is a sentimental, romantic little tune.* **Amanda** *hears him, and clutches at her throat suddenly as though she were suffocating. Then she jumps up noiselessly, and peers over the line of tubs.* **Elyot**, *with his back to her, continues to sing obliviously. She sits down again, relaxing with a gesture almost of despair. Then she looks anxiously over her shoulder at the window in case* **Victor** *should be listening, and then, with a little smile, she takes up the melody herself, clearly.* **Elyot** *stops dead and gives a gasp, then he jumps up, and stands looking at her. She continues to sing, pretending not to know that he is there. At the end of the song, she turns slowly, and faces him.*

Amanda   Thoughtful of them to play that, wasn't it?

Elyot   (*in a stifled voice*)   What are you doing here?

Amanda   I'm on honeymoon.

Elyot   How interesting, so am I.

Amanda   I hope you're enjoying it.

Elyot   It hasn't started yet.

Amanda   Neither has mine.

Elyot   Oh, my God!

Amanda   I can't help feeling that this is a little unfortunate.

Elyot   Are you happy?

Amanda   Perfectly.

Elyot   Good. That's all right, then, isn't it?

Amanda   Are you?

Elyot   Ecstatically.

Amanda   I'm delighted to hear it. We shall probably meet again sometime. Au revoir! (*She turns.*)

Elyot (*firmly*)   Good-bye.

She goes without looking back. He stands gazing after her with an expression of horror on his face. **Sibyl** *comes brightly on to the terrace in a very pretty evening frock.*

Sibyl   Cocktail, please. (**Elyot** *doesn't answer.*) Elli, what's the matter?

Elyot   I feel very odd.

Sibyl   Odd, what do you mean, Ill?

Elyot   Yes, ill.

Sibyl (*alarmed*)   What sort of –

Elyot   We must leave at once.

Sibyl   Leave!

Elyot   Yes, dear. Leave immediately.

Sibyl   Elli!

Elyot   I have a strange foreboding.

Sibyl   You must be mad.

Elyot   Listen, darling. I want you to be very sweet, and patient, and understanding, and not be upset, or ask any questions, or anything. I have an absolute conviction that our whole future happiness depends upon our leaving here instantly.

Sibyl Why?

Elyot I can't tell you why.

Sibyl But we've only just come.

Elyot I know that, but it can't be helped.

Sibyl What's happened, what has happened?

Elyot Nothing has happened.

Sibyl You've gone out of your mind.

Elyot I haven't gone out of my mind, but I shall if we stay here another hour.

Sibyl You're not drunk, are you?

Elyot Of course I'm not drunk. What time have I had to get drunk?

Sibyl Come down and have some dinner, darling, and then you'll feel ever so much better.

Elyot It's no use trying to humour me. I'm serious.

Sibyl But darling, please be reasonable. We've only just arrived; everything's unpacked. It's our first night together. We can't go away now.

Elyot We can have our first night together in Paris.

Sibyl We shouldn't get there until the small hours.

Elyot (*with a great effort at calmness*) Now please, Sibyl, I know it sounds crazy to you, and utterly lacking in reason and sense, but I've got second sight over certain things. I'm almost psychic. I've got the most extraordinary sensation of impending disaster. If we stay here something appalling will happen. I know it.

Sibyl (*firmly*) Hysterical nonsense.

Elyot It isn't hysterical nonsense. Presentiments are far from being nonsense. Look at the woman who cancelled her passage on the *Titanic*. All because of a presentiment.

Sibyl I don't see what that has to do with it.

Elyot It has everything to do with it. She obeyed her instincts, that's what she did, and saved her life. All I ask is to be allowed to obey my instinct.

Sibyl Do you mean that there's going to be an earthquake or something?

Elyot Very possibly, very possibly indeed, or perhaps a violent explosion.

Sibyl They don't have earthquakes in France.

Elyot On the contrary, only the other day they felt a distinct shock at Toulon.

Sibyl Yes, but that's in the South where it's hot.

Elyot Don't quibble, Sibyl.

Sibyl And as for explosions, there's nothing here that can explode.

Elyot Oho, isn't there.

Sibyl Yes, but Elli –

Elyot Darling, be sweet. Bear with me. I beseech you to bear with me.

Sibyl I don't understand. It's horrid of you to do this.

Elyot I'm not doing anything. I'm only asking you, imploring you to come away from this place.

Sibyl But I love it here.

Elyot There are thousands of other places far nicer.

Sibyl It's a pity we didn't go to one of them.

Elyot Now, listen, Sibyl –

Sibyl Yes, but why are you behaving like this, why, why, why?

Elyot   Don't ask why. Just give in to me. I swear I'll never ask you to give into me over anything again.

Sibyl (*with complete decision*)   I won't think of going tonight. It's utterly ridiculous. I've done quite enough travelling for one day, and I'm tired.

Elyot   You're as obstinate as a mule.

Sibyl   I like that, I must say.

Elyot (*hotly*)   You've got your nasty little feet dug into the ground, and you don't intend to budge an inch, do you?

Sibyl (*with spirit*)   No, I do not.

Elyot   If there's one thing in the world that infuriates me, it's sheer wanton stubbornness. I should like to cut off your head with a meat axe.

Sibyl   How dare you talk to me like that, on our honeymoon night.

Elyot   Damn our honeymoon night. Damn it, damn it, damn it!

Sibyl (*bursting into tears*)   Oh, Elli, Elli –

Elyot   Stop crying. Will you or will you not come away with me to Paris?

Sibyl   I've never been so miserable in my life. You're hateful and beastly. Mother was perfectly right. She said you had shifty eyes.

Elyot   Well, she can't talk. Hers are so close together, you couldn't put a needle between them.

Sibyl   You don't love me a little bit. I wish I were dead.

Elyot   Will you or will you not come to Paris?

Sibyl   No, no I won't.

Elyot   Oh, my God! (*He stamps indoors.*)

Sibyl (*following him, wailing*)   Oh, Elli, Elli, Elli –

Victor *comes stamping out of the French windows on the left, followed by* **Amanda**.

Victor You were certainly right when you said you weren't normal. You're behaving like a lunatic.

Amanda Not at all. All I have done is to ask you a little favour.

Victor Little favour indeed.

Amanda If we left now we could be in Paris in a few hours.

Victor If we crossed Siberia by train we could be in China in a fortnight, but I don't see any reason to do it.

Amanda Oh, Victor darling – please, please – be sensible, just for my sake.

Victor Sensible!

Amanda Yes, sensible. I shall be absolutely miserable if we stay here. You don't want me to be absolutely miserable all through my honeymoon, do you?

Victor But why on earth didn't you think of your sister's tragedy before?

Amanda I forgot.

Victor You couldn't forget a thing like that.

Amanda I got the places muddled. Then when I saw the Casino there in the moonlight, it all came back to me.

Victor When did all this happen?

Amanda Years ago, but it might just as well have been yesterday. I can see her now lying dead, with that dreadful expression on her face. Then all that awful business of taking the body home to England. It was perfectly horrible.

Victor I never knew you had a sister.

Amanda I haven't any more.

Victor There's something behind all this.

Amanda   Don't be silly. What could there be behind it?

Victor   Well, for one thing, I know you're lying.

Amanda   Victor!

Victor   Be honest. Aren't you?

Amanda   I can't think how you can be so mean and suspicious.

Victor (*patiently*)   You're lying, Amanda. Aren't you?

Amanda   Yes, Victor.

Victor   You never had a sister, dead or alive?

Amanda   I believe there was a stillborn one in 1902.

Victor   What is your reason for all this?

Amanda   I told you I was unreliable.

Victor   Why do you want to leave so badly?

Amanda   You'll be angry if I tell you the truth.

Victor   What is it?

Amanda   I warn you.

Victor   Tell me. Please tell me.

Amanda   Elyot's here.

Victor   What!

Amanda   I saw him.

Victor   When?

Amanda   Just now, when you were in the bath.

Victor   Where was he?

Amanda (*hesitatingly*)   Down there, in a white suit. (*She points over the balustrade.*)

Victor (*sceptically*)   White suit?

Amanda   Why not? It's summer, isn't it?

Victor   You're lying again.

Amanda   I'm not. He's here. I swear he is.

Victor   Well, what of it?

Amanda   I can't enjoy a honeymoon with you, with Elyot liable to bounce in at any moment.

Victor   Really, Mandy.

Amanda   Can't you see how awful it is? It's the most embarrassing thing that ever happened to me in my whole life.

Victor   Did he see you?

Amanda   No, he was running.

Victor   What was he running for?

Amanda   How on earth do I know. Don't be so annoying.

Victor   Well, as long as he didn't see you it's all right, isn't it?

Amanda   It isn't all right at all. We must leave immediately.

Victor   But why?

Amanda   How can you be so appallingly obstinate.

Victor   I'm not afraid of him.

Amanda   Neither am I. It isn't a question of being afraid. It's just a horrible awkward situation.

Victor   I'm damned if I can see why our whole honeymoon should be upset by Elyot.

Amanda   My last one was.

Victor   I don't believe he's here at all.

Amanda   He is I tell you. I saw him.

Victor   It was probably an optical illusion. This half light is very deceptive.

Amanda   It is no such thing.

Victor   I absolutely refuse to change all our plans at the last moment, just because you think you've seen Elyot. It's unreasonable and ridiculous of you to demand it. Even if he is here I can't see that it matters. He'll probably feel much more embarrassed than you, and a damned good job too; and if he annoys you in any way I'll knock him down.

Amanda That would be charming.

Victor Now don't let's talk about it any more.

Amanda Do you mean to stand there seriously and imagine that the whole thing can be glossed over as easily as that?

Victor I'm not going to leave, Mandy. If I start giving into you as early as this, our lives will be unbearable.

Amanda (*outraged*) Victor!

Victor (*calmly*) You've worked yourself up into a state over a situation which really only exists in your mind.

Amanda (*controlling herself with an effort*) Please, Victor, please, for this last time I implore you. Let's go to Paris now, to-night. I
mean it with all my heart – please –

Victor (*with gentle firmness*) No, Mandy!

Amanda I see quite clearly that I have been foolish enough to marry a fat old gentleman in a club armchair.

Victor It's no use being cross.

Amanda You're a pompous ass.

Victor (*horrified*) Mandy!

Amanda (*enraged*) Pompous ass, that's what I said, and that's what I meant. Blown out with your own importance.

Victor Mandy, control yourself.

Amanda Get away from me. I can't bear to think I'm married to such rugged grandeur.

Victor (*with great dignity*) I shall be in the bar. When you are ready to come down and dine, let me know.

Amanda (*flinging herself into a chair*) Go away, go away.

Victor *stalks off, at the same moment that* **Elyot** *stamps on, on the other side, followed by* **Sibyl** *in tears.*

Elyot If you don't stop screaming, I'll murder you.

Sibyl I wish to heaven I'd never seen you in my life, let alone married you. I don't wonder Amanda left you, if you behaved to her as you've behaved to me. I'm going down to have dinner by myself and you can just do what you like about it.

Elyot Do, and I hope it chokes you.

Sibyl Oh Elli, Elli –

She goes wailing indoors. **Elyot** *stamps down to the balustrade and lights a cigarette, obviously trying to control his nerves.* **Amanda** *sees him, and comes down too.*

Amanda Give me one for God's sake.

Elyot (*hands her his case laconically*) Here.

Amanda (*taking a cigarette*) I'm in such a rage.

Elyot (*lighting up*) So am I.

Amanda What are we to do?

Elyot I don't know.

Amanda Whose yacht is that?

Elyot The Duke of Westminster's, I expect. It always is.

Amanda I wish I were on it.

Elyot I wish you were too.

Amanda There's no need to be nasty.

Elyot Yes there is, every need. I've never in my life felt a greater urge to be nasty.

Amanda And you've had some urges in your time, haven't you?

Elyot If you start bickering with me, Amanda, I swear I'll throw you over the edge.

Amanda   Try it, that's all, just try it.

Elyot   You've upset everything, as usual.

Amanda   I've upset everything! What about you?

Elyot   Ever since the first moment I was unlucky enough to set eyes on you, my life has been insupportable.

Amanda   Oh do shut up, there's no sense in going on like that.

Elyot   Nothing's any use. There's no escape, ever.

Amanda   Don't be melodramatic.

Elyot   Do you want a cocktail? There are two here.

Amanda   There are two over here as well.

Elyot   We'll have my two first.

Amanda   *crosses over into* **Elyot***'s part of the terrace. He gives her one, and keeps one himself.*

Amanda   Shall we get roaring screaming drunk?

Elyot   I don't think that would help, we did it once before and it was a dismal failure.

Amanda   It was lovely at the beginning.

Elyot   You have an immoral memory, Amanda. Here's to you. (*They raise their glasses solemnly and drink.*)

Amanda   I tried to get away the moment after I'd seen you, but he wouldn't budge.

Elyot   What's his name.

Amanda   Victor, Victor Prynne.

Elyot (*toasting*)   Mr and Mrs Victor Prynne. (*He drinks.*) Mine wouldn't budge either.

Amanda   What's her name?

Elyot   Sibyl.

Amanda (*toasting*)   Mr and Mrs Elyot Chase. (*She drinks.*) God pity the poor girl.

Elyot   Are you in love with him?

Amanda   Of course.

Elyot   How funny.

Amanda   I don't see anything particularly funny about it, you're in love with yours, aren't you?

Elyot   Certainly.

Amanda   There you are then.

Elyot   There we both are then.

Amanda   What's she like?

Elyot   Fair, very pretty, plays the piano beautifully.

Amanda   Very comforting.

Elyot   How's yours?

Amanda   I don't want to discuss him.

Elyot   Well, it doesn't matter, he'll probably come popping out in a minute and I shall see for myself. Does he know I'm here?

Amanda   Yes, I told him.

Elyot (*with sarcasm*)   That's going to make things a whole lot easier.

Amanda   You needn't be frightened, he won't hurt you.

Elyot   If he comes near me I'll scream the place down.

Amanda   Does Sibyl know I'm here?

Elyot   No, I pretended I'd had a presentiment. I tried terribly hard to persuade her to leave for Paris.

Amanda   I tried too, it's lucky we didn't both succeed, isn't it? Otherwise we should probably all have joined up in Rouen or somewhere.

Elyot (*laughing*)   In some frowsy little hotel.

Amanda (*laughing too*)   Oh dear, it would have been much, much worse.

Elyot   I can see us all sailing down in the morning for an early start.

Amanda (*weakly*)   Lovely, oh lovely.

Elyot   Glorious! (*They both laugh helplessly.*)

Amanda   What's happened to yours?

Elyot   Didn't you hear her screaming? She's downstairs in the dining-room I think.

Amanda   Mine is being grand, in the bar.

Elyot   It really is awfully difficult.

Amanda   Have you known her long?

Elyot   About four months, we met in a house party in Norfolk.

Amanda   Very flat, Norfolk.

Elyot   How old is dear Victor?

Amanda   Thirty-four, or five; and Sibyl?

Elyot   I blush to tell you, only twenty-three.

Amanda   You've gone a mucker all right.

Elyot   I shall reserve my opinion of your choice until I've met dear Victor.

Amanda   I wish you wouldn't go on calling him 'Dear Victor'. It's extremely irritating.

Elyot   That's how I see him. Dumpy, and fair, and very considerate, with glasses. Dear Victor.

Amanda   As I said before I would rather not discuss him. At least I have good taste enough to refrain from making cheap gibes at Sibyl.

Elyot   You said Norfolk was flat.

Amanda That was no reflection on her, unless she made it flatter.

Elyot Your voice takes on an acid quality whenever you mention her name.

Amanda I'll never mention it again.

Elyot Good, and I'll keep off Victor.

Amanda (*with dignity*) Thank you.

There is silence for a moment. The orchestra starts playing the same tune that they were singing previously.

Elyot That orchestra has a remarkably small repertoire.

Amanda They don't seem to know anything but this, do they?

She sits down on the balustrade, and sings it, softly. Her eyes are looking out to sea, and her mind is far away. **Elyot** *watches her while she sings. When she turns to him at the end, there are tears in her eyes. He looks away awkwardly and lights another cigarette.*

Elyot You always had a sweet voice, Amanda.

Amanda (*a little huskily*) Thank you.

Elyot I'm awfully sorry about all this, really I am. I wouldn't have had it happen for the world.

Amanda I know. I'm sorry too. It's just rotten luck.

Elyot I'll go away to-morrow whatever happens, so don't you worry.

Amanda That's nice of you.

Elyot I hope everything turns out splendidly for you, and that you'll be very happy.

Amanda I hope the same for you, too.

The music, which has been playing continually through this little scene, returns persistently to the refrain. They both look at one another and laugh.

Elyot Nasty insistent little tune.

Amanda   Extraordinary how potent cheap music is.

Elyot   What exactly were you remembering at that moment?

Amanda   The Palace Hotel Skating Rink in the morning, bright strong sunlight, and everybody whirling round in vivid colours, and you kneeling down to put on my skates for me.

Elyot   You'd fallen on your fanny a few moments before.

Amanda   It was beastly of you to laugh like that, I felt so humiliated.

Elyot   Poor darling.

Amanda   Do you remember waking up in the morning, and standing on the balcony, looking out across the valley?

Elyot   Blue shadows on white snow, cleanness beyond belief, high above everything in the world. How beautiful it was.

Amanda   It's nice to think we had a few marvellous moments.

Elyot   A few: We had heaps really, only they slip away into the background, and one only remembers the bad ones.

Amanda   Yes. What fools we were to ruin it all. What utter, utter fools.

Elyot   You feel like that too, do you?

Amanda (*wearily*)   Of course.

Elyot   Why did we?

Amanda   The whole business was too much for us.

Elyot   We were so ridiculously over in love.

Amanda   Funny wasn't it?

Elyot (*sadly*)   Horribly funny.

Amanda   Selfishness, cruelty, hatred, possessiveness, petty jealousy. All those qualities came out in us just because we loved each other.

Elyot Perhaps they were there anyhow.

Amanda No, it's love that does it. To hell with love.

Elyot To hell with love.

Amanda And yet here we are starting afresh with two quite different people. In love all over again, aren't we? (**Elyot** *doesn't answer.*) Aren't we?

Elyot No.

Amanda Elyot.

Elyot We're not in love all over again, and you know it. Good night, Amanda. (*He turns abruptly, and goes towards the French windows.*)

Amanda Elyot – don't be silly – come back.

Elyot I must go and find Sibyl.

Amanda I must go and find Victor.

Elyot (*savagely*) Well, why don't you?

Amanda I don't want to.

Elyot It's shameful, shameful of us.

Amanda Don't: I feel terrible. Don't leave me for a minute, I shall go mad if you do. We won't talk about ourselves any more, we'll talk about outside things, anything you like, only just don't leave me until I've pulled myself together.

Elyot Very well. (*There is a dead silence.*)

Amanda What have you been doing lately? During these last years?

Elyot Travelling about. I went round the world, you know, after –

Amanda (*hurriedly*) Yes, yes, I know. How was it?

Elyot The world?

Amanda Yes.

Elyot   Oh, highly enjoyable.

Amanda   China must be very interesting.

Elyot   Very big, China.

Amanda   And Japan –

Elyot   Very small.

Amanda   Did you eat sharks' fins, and take your shoes off, and use chopsticks and everything?

Elyot   Practically everything.

Amanda   And India, the burning Ghars, or Ghats, or whatever they are, and the Taj Mahal. How was the Taj Mahal?

Elyot (*looking at her*)   Unbelievable, a sort of dream.

Amanda   That was the moonlight, I expect, you must have seen it in the moonlight.

Elyot (*never taking his eyes off her face*)   Yes, moonlight is cruelly deceptive.

Amanda   And it didn't look like a biscuit box, did it? I've always felt that it might.

Elyot (*quietly*)   Darling, darling, I love you so.

Amanda   And I do hope you met a sacred Elephant. They're lint white, I believe, and very, very sweet.

Elyot   I've never loved anyone else for an instant.

Amanda (*raising her hand feebly in protest*)   No, no, you mustn't – Elyot – stop.

Elyot   You love me, too, don't you? There's no doubt about it anywhere, is there?

Amanda   No, no doubt anywhere.

Elyot   You're looking very lovely, you know, in this damned moonlight. Your skin is clear and cool, and your eyes are shining, and you're growing lovelier and lovelier every second as I look at you. You don't hold any mystery for me, darling, do you mind? There isn't a particle of you that I don't know, remember, and want.

Amanda (*softly*) I'm glad, my sweet.

Elyot More than any desire anywhere, deep down in my deepest heart I want you back again – please –

Amanda (*putting her hand over his mouth*) Don't say any more, you're making me cry so dreadfully.

He pulls her gently into his arms and they stand silently, completely oblivious to everything but the moment, and each other. When, finally, they separate, they sit down, rather breathlessly, on the balustrade.

Amanda What now? Oh darling, what now?

Elyot I don't know, I'm lost, utterly.

Amanda We must think quickly, oh quickly –

Elyot Escape?

Amanda Together?

Elyot Yes, of course, now, now.

Amanda We can't, we can't, you know we can't.

Elyot We must.

Amanda It would break Victor's heart.

Elyot And Sibyl's too probably, but they're bound to suffer anyhow. Think of the hell we'd lead them into if we stayed. Infinitely worse than any cruelty in the world, pretending to love them, and loving each other, so desperately.

Amanda We must tell them.

Elyot What?

Amanda Call them, and tell them.

Elyot Oh no, no, that's impossible.

Amanda It's honest.

Elyot I can't help how honest it is, it's too horrible to think of. How should we start? What should we say?

Amanda We should have to trust to the inspiration of the moment.

Elyot It would be a moment completely devoid of inspiration. The most appalling moment imaginable. No, no, we can't, you must see that, we simply can't.

Amanda What do you propose to do then? As it is they might appear at any moment.

Elyot We've got to decide instantly one way or another. Go away together now, or stay with them, and never see one another again, ever.

Amanda Don't be silly, what choice is there?

Elyot No choice at all, come – (*He takes her hand.*)

Amanda No, wait. This is sheer raving madness, something's happened to us, we're not sane.

Elyot We never were.

Amanda Where can we go?

Elyot Paris first, my car's in the garage, all ready.

Amanda They'll follow us.

Elyot That doesn't matter, once the thing's done.

Amanda I've got a flat in Paris.

Elyot Good.

Amanda It's in the Avenue Montaigne. I let it to Freda Lawson, but she's in Biarritz, so it's empty.

Elyot Does Victor know?

Amanda No, he knows I have one but he hasn't the faintest idea where.

Elyot   Better and better.

Amanda   We're being so bad, so terribly bad, we'll suffer for this, I know we shall.

Elyot   Can't be helped.

Amanda   Starting all those awful rows all over again.

Elyot   No, no, we're older and wiser now.

Amanda   What difference does that make? The first moment either of us gets a bit nervy, off we'll go again.

Elyot   Stop shilly-shallying, Amanda.

Amanda   I'm trying to be sensible.

Elyot   You're only succeeding in being completely idiotic.

Amanda   Idiotic indeed! What about you?

Elyot   Now look here, Amanda –

Amanda (*stricken*)   Oh my God!

Elyot (*rushing to her and kissing her*)   Darling, darling, I didn't mean it –

Amanda   I won't move from here unless we have a compact, a sacred, sacred compact never to quarrel again.

Elyot   Easy to make but difficult to keep.

Amanda   No, no, it's the bickering that always starts it. The moment we notice we're bickering, either of us, we must promise on our honour to stop dead. We'll invent some phrase or catchword, which when either of us says it, automatically cuts off all conversation for at least five minutes.

Elyot   Two minutes dear, with an option of renewal.

Amanda   Very well, what shall it be?

Elyot (*hurriedly*)   Solomon Isaacs.

Amanda   All right, that'll do.

Elyot   Come on, come on.

Amanda   What shall we do if we meet either of them on the way downstairs?

Elyot   Run like stags.

Amanda   What about clothes?

Elyot   I've got a couple of bags I haven't unpacked yet.

Amanda   I've got a small trunk.

Elyot   Send the porter up for it.

Amanda   Oh this is terrible – terrible –

Elyot   Come on, come on, don't waste time.

Amanda   Oughtn't we to leave notes or something?

Elyot   No, no, no, we'll telegraph from somewhere on the road.

Amanda   Darling, I daren't, it's too wicked of us, I simply daren't:

Elyot (*seizing her in his arms and kissing her violently*)   Now will you behave?

Amanda   Yes, but Elyot darling –

Elyot   Solomon Isaacs!

They rush off together through **Elyot**'*s suite. After a moment or so* **Victor** *steps out on to the terrace and looks round anxiously. Then he goes back indoors again, and can be heard calling* '**Mandy**'. *Finally he again comes out on to the terrace and comes despondently down to the balustrade. He hears* **Sibyl**'*s voice calling* '**Elli**' *and looks round as she comes out of the French windows. She jumps slightly upon seeing him.*

Victor   Good evening.

Sibyl (*rather flustered*)   Good evening – I was – er – looking for my husband.

Victor   Really, that's funny. I was looking for my wife.

Sibyl   Quite a coincidence. (*She laughs nervously.*)

Victor (*after a pause*)   It's very nice here, isn't it?

Sibyl   Lovely.

Victor   Have you been here long?

Sibyl   No, we only arrived today.

Victor   Another coincidence. So did we.

Sibyl   How awfully funny.

Victor   Would you care for a cocktail?

Sibyl   Oh no thank you – really –

Victor   There are two here on the table.

Sibyl *glances at the two empty glasses on the balustrade, and tosses her head defiantly.*

Sibyl   Thanks very much, I'd love one.

Victor   Good, here you are. (**Sibyl** *comes over to* **Victor***'s side of the terrace. He hands her one and takes one himself.*)

Sibyl   Thank you.

Victor (*with rather forced gaiety*)   To absent friends. (*He raises his glass.*)

Sibyl (*raising hers*)   To absent friends. (*They both laugh rather mirthlessly and then sit down on the balustrade, pensively sipping their cocktails and looking at the view.*) It's awfully pretty, isn't it? The moonlight, and the lights of that yacht reflected in the water –

Victor   I wonder who it belongs to.

The curtain slowly falls.

Act Two

The scene is **Amanda***'s flat in Paris. A few days have elapsed since Act One. The flat is charmingly furnished, its principal features being a Steinway Grand on the left, facing slightly up-stage. Down-stage centre, a very large comfortable sofa, behind which is a small table. There is also another sofa somewhere about, and one or two small tables, and a gramophone. The rest can be left to the discretion and taste of the decorator.*

When the curtain rises it is about ten o'clock in the evening. The windows are wide open, and the various street sounds of Paris can be heard but not very loudly as the apartment is high up.

Amanda *and* **Elyot** *are seated opposite one another at the table. They have finished dinner and are dallying over coffee and liqueurs.* **Amanda** *is wearing pyjamas, and* **Elyot** *a comfortable dressing-gown.*

Amanda   I'm glad we let Louise go. I am afraid she is going to have a cold.

Elyot   Going to have a cold; she's been grunting and snorting all the evening like a whole herd of Bison.

Amanda (*thoughtfully*)   Bison never sounds right to me somehow. I have a feeling it ought to be Bisons, a flock of Bisons.

Elyot   You might say a covey of Bisons, or even a school of Bisons.

Amanda   Yes, lovely. The Royal London School of Bisons. Do you think Louise is happy at home?

Elyot   No, profoundly miserable.

Amanda   Family beastly to her?

Elyot (*with conviction*)   Absolutely vile. Knock her about dreadfully, I expect, make her eat the most disgusting food, and pull her fringe.

Amanda (*laughing*) Oh, poor Louise.

Elyot Well, you know what the French are.

Amanda Oh yes, indeed. I know what the Hungarians are too.

Elyot What are they?

Amanda Very wistful. It's all those Pretzels I shouldn't wonder.

Elyot And the Poostza; I always felt the Poostza was far too big, Danube or no Danube.

Amanda Have you ever crossed the Sahara on a camel?

Elyot Frequently. When I was a boy we used to do it all the time. My grandmother had a lovely seat on a camel.

Amanda There's no doubt about it, foreign travel's the thing.

Elyot Would you like some brandy?

Amanda Just a little. (*He pours some into her glass and some into his own.*)

Elyot I'm glad we didn't go out to-night.

Amanda Or last night.

Elyot Or the night before.

Amanda There's no reason to, really, when we're cosy here.

Elyot Exactly.

Amanda It's nice, isn't it?

Elyot Strangely peaceful. It's an awfully bad reflection on our characters. We ought to be absolutely tortured with conscience.

Amanda We are, every now and then.

Elyot Not nearly enough.

Amanda   We sent Victor and Sibyl a nice note from wherever it was, what more can they want?

Elyot   You're even more ruthless than I am.

Amanda   I don't believe in crying over my bridge before I've eaten it.

Elyot   Very sensible.

Amanda   Personally I feel grateful for a miraculous escape. I know now that I should never have been happy with Victor. I was a fool ever to consider it.

Elyot   You did a little more than consider it.

Amanda   Well, you can't talk.

Elyot   I wonder whether they met each other, or whether they've been suffering alone.

Amanda   Oh dear, don't let's go on about it, it really does make one feel rather awful.

Elyot   I suppose one or other or both of them will turn up here eventually.

Amanda   Bound to; it won't be very nice, will it?

Elyot (*cheerfully*)   Perfectly horrible.

Amanda   Do you realise that we're living in sin?

Elyot   Not according to the Catholics, Catholics don't recognise divorce. We're married as much as ever we were.

Amanda   Yes, dear, but we're not Catholics.

Elyot   Never mind, it's nice to think they'd sort of back us up. We were married in the eyes of heaven, and we still are.

Amanda   We may be all right in the eyes of Heaven, but we look like being in the hell of a mess socially.

Elyot   Who cares?

Amanda   Are we going to marry again, after Victor and Sibyl divorce us?

Elyot I suppose so. What do you think?

Amanda I feel rather scared of marriage really.

Elyot It is a frowsy business.

Amanda I believe it was just the fact of our being married, and clamped together publicly, that wrecked us before.

Elyot That, and not knowing how to manage each other.

Amanda Do you think we know how to manage each other now?

Elyot This week's been very successful. We've hardly used Solomon Isaacs at all.

Amanda Solomon Isaacs is so long, let's shorten it to Sollocks.

Elyot All right.

Amanda Darling, you do look awfully sweet in your little dressing-gown.

Elyot Yes, it's pretty ravishing, isn't it?

Amanda Do you mind if I come round and kiss you?

Elyot A pleasure, Lady Agatha.

Amanda *comes round the table, kisses him, picks up the coffee pot, and returns to her chair.*

Amanda What fools we were to subject ourselves to five years' unnecessary suffering.

Elyot Perhaps it wasn't unnecessary, perhaps it mellowed and perfected us like beautiful ripe fruit.

Amanda When we were together, did you really think I was unfaithful to you?

Elyot Yes, practically every day.

Amanda I thought you were too; often I used to torture

myself with visions of your bouncing about on divans with awful widows.

Elyot   Why widows?

Amanda   I was thinking of Claire Lavenham really.

Elyot   Oh Claire.

Amanda (*sharply*)   What did you say 'Oh Claire' like that for? It sounded far too careless to me.

Elyot (*wistfully*)   What a lovely creature she was.

Amanda   Lovely, lovely, lovely!

Elyot (*blowing her a kiss*)   Darling!

Amanda   Did you ever have an affair with her? Afterwards I mean?

Elyot   Why do you want to know?

Amanda   Curiosity, I suppose.

Elyot   Dangerous.

Amanda   Oh not now, not dangerous now. I wouldn't expect you to have been celibate during those five years, any more than I was.

Elyot (*jumping*)   What?

Amanda   After all, Claire was undeniably attractive. A trifle over-vivacious I always thought, but that was probably because she was fundamentally stupid.

Elyot   What do you mean about not being celibate during those five years?

Amanda   What do you think I mean?

Elyot   Oh God! (*He looks down miserably.*)

Amanda   What's the matter?

Elyot   You know perfectly well what's the matter.

Amanda (*gently*)   You mustn't be unreasonable, I was only trying to stamp out the memory of you. I expect your affairs well outnumbered mine anyhow.

Elyot   That is a little different. I'm a man.

Amanda   Excuse me a moment while I get a caraway biscuit and change my crinoline.

Elyot   It doesn't suit women to be promiscuous.

Amanda   It doesn't suit men for women to be promiscuous.

Elyot (*with sarcasm*)   Very modern, dear; really your advanced views quite startle me.

Amanda   Don't be cross, Elyot, I haven't been so dreadfully loose actually. Five years is a long time, and even if I did nip off with someone every now and again, they were none of them very serious.

Elyot (*rising from the table and walking away*)   Oh, do stop it please –

Amanda   Well, what about you?

Elyot   Do you want me to tell you?

Amanda   No, no, I don't – I take everything back – I don't.

Elyot (*viciously*)   I was madly in love with a woman in South Africa.

Amanda   Did she have a ring through her nose?

Elyot   Don't be revolting.

Amanda   We're tormenting one another. Sit down, sweet, I'm scared.

Elyot (*slowly*)   Very well. (*He sits down thoughtfully.*)

Amanda   We should have said Sollocks ages ago.

Elyot   We're in love all right.

Amanda   Don't say it so bitterly. Let's try to get the best out of it this time, instead of the worst.

Elyot (*stretching his hand across the table*) Hand please.

Amanda (*clasping it*) Here.

Elyot More comfortable?

Amanda Much more.

Elyot (*after a slight pause*) Are you engaged for this dance?

Amanda Funnily enough I was, but my partner was suddenly taken ill.

Elyot (*rising and going to the gramophone*) It's this damned smallpox epidemic.

Amanda No, as a matter of fact it was kidney trouble.

Elyot You'll dance it with me, I hope?

Amanda (*rising*) I shall be charmed.

Elyot (*as they dance*) Quite a good floor, isn't it?

Amanda Yes, I think it needs a little Borax.

Elyot I love Borax.

Amanda Is that the Grand Duchess Olga lying under the piano?

Elyot Yes, her husband died a few weeks ago, you know, on his way from Pulborough. So sad.

Amanda What on earth was he doing in Pulborough?

Elyot Nobody knows exactly, but there have been the usual stories.

Amanda I see.

Elyot Delightful parties Lady Bundle always gives, doesn't she?

Amanda Entrancing. Such a dear old lady.

Elyot And so gay: Did you notice her at supper blowing all those shrimps through her ear trumpet?

The tune comes to an end. **Amanda** *sits on the edge of the sofa, pensively.*

Elyot What are you thinking about?

Amanda Nothing in particular.

Elyot Come on, I know that face.

Amanda Poor Sibyl.

Elyot Sibyl?

Amanda Yes, I suppose she loves you terribly.

Elyot Not as much as all that, she didn't have a chance to get really under way.

Amanda I expect she's dreadfully unhappy.

Elyot Oh, do shut up, Amanda, we've had all that out before.

Amanda We've certainly been pretty busy trying to justify ourselves.

Elyot It isn't a question of justifying ourselves, it's the true values of the situation that are really important. The moment we saw one another again we knew it was no use going on. We knew it instantly really, although we tried to pretend to ourselves that we didn't. What we've got to be thankful for is that we made the break straight away and not later.

Amanda You think we should have done it anyhow?

Elyot Of course, and things would have been in a worse mess than they are now.

Amanda And what if we'd never happened to meet again. Would you have been quite happy with Sibyl?

Elyot I expect so.

Amanda Oh, Elyot!

Elyot You needn't look so stricken. It would have been the same with you and Victor. Life would have been smooth, and amicable, and quite charming, wouldn't it?

Amanda   Poor dear Victor. He certainly did love me.

Elyot   Splendid.

Amanda   When I met him I was so lonely and depressed, I felt that I was getting old, and crumbling away unwanted.

Elyot   It certainly is horrid when one begins to crumble.

Amanda (*wistfully*)   He used to look at me hopelessly like a lovely spaniel, and I sort of melted like snow in the sunlight.

Elyot   That must have been an edifying spectacle.

Amanda   Victor really had a great charm

Elyot   You must tell me all about it.

Amanda   He had a positive mania for looking after me, and protecting me.

Elyot   That would have died down in time, dear.

Amanda   You mustn't be rude, there's no necessity to be rude.

Elyot   I wasn't in the least rude, I merely made a perfectly rational statement.

Amanda   Your voice was decidedly bitter.

Elyot   Victor had glorious legs, hadn't he? And fascinating ears.

Amanda   Don't be silly.

Elyot   He probably looked radiant in the morning, all flushed and tumbled on the pillow.

Amanda   I never saw him on the pillow.

Elyot   I'm surprised to hear it.

Amanda (*angrily*)   Elyot!

Elyot   There's no need to be cross.

Amanda What did you mean by that?

Elyot I'm sick of listening to you yap, yap, yap, yap, yap, yapping about Victor.

Amanda Now listen, Elyot, once and for all –

Elyot Oh my dear, Sollocks! Sollocks! – two minutes – Sollocks.

Amanda But –

Elyot (*firmly*) Sollocks!

They sit in dead silence, looking at each other. **Amanda** *makes a sign that she wants a cigarette.* **Elyot** *gets up, hands her the box, and lights one for her and himself.* **Amanda** *rises and walks over to the window, and stands there, looking out for a moment. Presently* **Elyot** *joins her. They draw the curtains and then come down and sit side by side on the sofa.* **Elyot** *looks at his watch.* **Amanda** *raises her eyebrows at him and he nods, then they both sigh, audibly.*

Elyot That was a near thing.

Amanda It was my fault. I'm terribly sorry, darling.

Elyot I was very irritating, I know I was. I'm sure Victor was awfully nice, and you're perfectly right to be sweet about him.

Amanda That's downright handsome of you. Sweetheart! (*She kisses him.*)

Elyot (*leaning back with her on the sofa*) I think I love you more than ever before. Isn't it ridiculous? Put your feet up.

She puts her legs across his, and they snuggle back together in the corner of the sofa, his head resting on her shoulder.

Amanda Comfortable?

Elyot Almost, wait a minute.

He struggles a bit and then settles down with a sigh.

Amanda How long, Oh Lord, how long?

Elyot (*drowsily*)   What do you mean, 'how long, Oh Lord, how long?'

Amanda   This is far too perfect to last.

Elyot   You have no faith, that's what's wrong with you.

Amanda   Absolutely none.

Elyot   Don't you believe in – ? (*He nods upwards.*)

Amanda   No, do you?

Elyot (*shaking his head*)   No. What about – ? (*He points downwards.*)

Amanda   Oh dear no.

Elyot   Don't you believe in anything?

Amanda   Oh yes, I believe in being kind to everyone, and giving money to old beggar women, and being as gay as possible.

Elyot   What about after we're dead?

Amanda   I think a rather gloomy merging into everything, don't you?

Elyot   I hope not, I'm a bad merger.

Amanda   You won't know a thing about it.

Elyot   I hope for a glorious oblivion, like being under gas.

Amanda   I always dream the most peculiar things under gas.

Elyot   Would you be young always? If you could choose?

Amanda   No, I don't think so, not if it meant having awful bull's glands popped into me.

Elyot   Cows for you, dear. Bulls for me.

Amanda   We certainly live in a marvellous age.

Elyot   Too marvellous. It's all right if you happen to be a specialist at something, then you're too concentrated to pay attention to all the other things going on. But, for the ordinary observer, it's too much.

Amanda (*snuggling closer*) Far, far too much.

Elyot Take the radio for instance.

Amanda Oh darling, don't let's take the radio.

Elyot Well, aeroplanes then, and Cosmic Atoms, and Television, and those gland injections we were talking about just now.

Amanda It must be so nasty for the poor animals, being experimented on.

Elyot Not when the experiments are successful. Why, in Vienna I believe you can see whole lines of decrepit old rats carrying on like Tiller Girls.

Amanda (*laughing*) Oh, how very, very sweet.

Elyot (*burying his face in her shoulder*) I do love you so.

Amanda Don't blow, dear heart, it gives me the shivers.

Elyot (*trying to kiss her*) Swivel your face round a bit more.

Amanda (*obliging*) That better?

Elyot (*kissing her lingeringly*) Very nice, thank you kindly.

Amanda (*twining her arm round his neck*) Darling, you're so terribly, terribly dear, and sweet, and attractive. (*She pulls his head down to her again and they kiss lovingly.*)

Elyot (*softly*) We were raving mad, ever to part, even for an instant.

Amanda Utter imbeciles.

Elyot I realised it almost immediately, didn't you?

Amanda Long before we got our decree.

Elyot My heart broke on that damned trip round the world. I saw such beautiful things, darling. Moonlight shining on old Temples, strange barbaric dances in jungle villages, scarlet flamingos flying over deep, deep blue water. Breathlessly lovely, and completely unexciting because you weren't there to see them with me.

Amanda (*kissing him again*)   Take me please, take me at once, let's make up for lost time.

Elyot   Next week?

Amanda   To-morrow.

Elyot   Done.

Amanda   I must see those dear Flamingos. (*There is a pause.*) Eight years all told, we've loved each other. Three married and five divorced.

Elyot   Angel. Angel. Angel. (*He kisses her passionately.*)

Amanda (*struggling slightly*)   No, Elyot, stop now, stop –

Elyot   Why should I stop? You know you adore being made love to.

Amanda (*through his kisses*)   It's so soon after dinner.

Elyot (*jumping up rather angrily*)   You really do say most awful things.

Amanda (*tidying her hair*)   I don't see anything particularly awful about that.

Elyot   No sense of glamour, no sense of glamour at all.

Amanda   It's difficult to feel really glamorous with a crick in the neck.

Elyot   Why didn't you say you had a crick in your neck?

Amanda (*sweetly*)   It's gone now.

Elyot   How convenient. (*He lights a cigarette.*)

Amanda (*holding out her hand*)   I want one please.

Elyot (*throwing her one*)   Here.

Amanda   Match?

Elyot (*impatiently*)   Wait a minute, can't you?

Amanda Chivalrous little love.

Elyot (*throwing the matches at her*) Here.

Amanda (*coldly*) Thank you very much indeed. (*There is a silence for a moment.*)

Elyot You really can be more irritating than anyone in the world.

Amanda I fail to see what I've done that's so terribly irritating.

Elyot You have no tact.

Amanda Tact. You have no consideration.

Elyot (*walking up and down*) Too soon after dinner indeed.

Amanda Yes, much too soon.

Elyot That sort of remark shows rather a common sort of mind, I'm afraid.

Amanda Oh it does, does it?

Elyot Very unpleasant, makes me shudder.

Amanda Making all this fuss just because your silly vanity is a little upset.

Elyot Vanity: What do you mean, vanity?

Amanda You can't bear the thought that there are certain moments when our chemical, what d'you call 'ems, don't fuse properly.

Elyot (*derisively*) Chemical what d'you call 'ems: Please try to be more explicit.

Amanda You know perfectly well what I mean, and don't you try to patronise me.

Elyot (*loudly*) Now look here, Amanda –

Amanda (*suddenly*) Darling Sollocks! Oh, for God's sake, Sollocks!

Elyot But listen –

Amanda Sollocks, Sollocks, Oh dear – triple Sollocks!

They stand looking at one another in silence for a moment, then **Amanda** *flings herself down on the sofa and buries her face in the cushions.* **Elyot** *looks at her, then goes over to the piano. He sits down and begins to play idly.* **Amanda** *raises her head, screws herself round on the sofa, and lies there listening.* **Elyot** *blows a kiss to her and goes on playing. He starts to sing softly to her, never taking his eyes off her. When he has finished the little refrain, whatever it was, he still continues to play it looking at her.*

Amanda Big romantic stuff, darling.

Elyot (*smiling*) Yes, big romantic stuff.

He wanders off into another tune. **Amanda** *sits up cross-legged on the sofa, and begins to sing it, then, still singing, she comes over and perches on the piano. They sing several old refrains from dead and gone musical comedies finishing with the song that brought them together again in the first Act. Finally* **Amanda** *comes down and sits next to him on the piano stool, they both therefore have their backs half turned to the audience. She rests her head on his shoulder, until finally his fingers drop off the keys, and they melt into one another's arms.*

Elyot (*after a moment*) You're the most thrilling, exciting woman that was ever born.

Amanda (*standing up, and brushing her hand lightly over his mouth*) Dearest, dearest heart –

He catches at her hand and kisses it, and then her arm, until he is standing up, embracing her ardently. She struggles a little, half laughing, and breaks away, but he catches her, and they finish up on the sofa again, clasped in each other's arms, both completely given up to the passion of the moment, until the telephone bell rings violently, and they both spring apart.

Elyot Good God!

Amanda Do you think it's them?

Elyot I wonder.

Amanda Nobody knows we're here except Freda, and

she wouldn't ring up.

Elyot   It must be them then.

Amanda   What are we to do?

Elyot (*suddenly*)   We're all right darling, aren't we –
whatever happens?

Amanda   Now and always, Sweet.

Elyot   I don't care then.

*He gets up and goes defiantly over to the telephone, which has been
ringing incessantly during the little preceding scene.*

Amanda   It was bound to come sooner or later.

Elyot (*at telephone*)   Hallo – hallo – what – comment?
Madame, qui? 'allo – 'allo – oui c'est ça. Oh, Madame
Duvallon – Oui, oui, oui. (*He puts his hand over the mouthpiece.*)
It's only somebody wanting to talk to the dear Madame
Duvallon.

Amanda   Who's she?

Elyot   I haven't the faintest idea. (*At telephone.*) Je regrette
beaucoup, Monsieur, mais Madame Duvallon viens de
partir – cette apres midi, pour Madagascar. (*He hangs up the
telephone.*) Whew; that gave me a fright.

Amanda   It sent shivers up my spine.

Elyot   What shall we do if they suddenly walk in on us?

Amanda   Behave exquisitely.

Elyot   With the most perfect poise?

Amanda   Certainly, I shall probably do a Court Curtsey.

Elyot (*sitting on the edge of the sofa*)   Things that ought to
matter dreadfully, don't matter at all when one's happy, do
they?

Amanda   What is so horrible is that one can't stay happy.

Elyot   Darling, don't say that.

Amanda   It's true. The whole business is a very poor joke.

Elyot   Meaning that sacred and beautiful thing, Love?

Amanda   Yes, meaning just that.

Elyot (*striding up and down the room dramatically*)   What does it all mean, that's what I ask myself in my ceaseless quest for ultimate truth. Dear God, what does it all mean?

Amanda   Don't laugh at me, I'm serious.

Elyot (*seriously*)   You mustn't be serious, my dear one, it's just what they want.

Amanda   Who's they?

Elyot   All the futile moralists who try to make life unbearable. Laugh at them. Be flippant. Laugh at everything, all their sacred shibboleths. Flippancy brings out the acid in their damned sweetness and light.

Amanda   If I laugh at everything, I must laugh at us too.

Elyot   Certainly you must. We're figures of fun all right.

Amanda   How long will it last, this ludicrous, overbearing love of ours?

Elyot   Who knows?

Amanda   Shall we always want to bicker and fight?

Elyot   No, that desire will fade, along with our passion.

Amanda   Oh dear, shall we like that?

Elyot   It all depends on how well we've played.

Amanda   What happens if one of us dies? Does the one that's left still laugh?

Elyot   Yes, yes, with all his might.

Amanda (*wistfully clutching his hand*)   That's serious enough, isn't it?

Elyot   No, no, it isn't. Death's very laughable, such a cunning little mystery. All done with mirrors.

Amanda Darling, I believe you're talking nonsense.

Elyot So is everyone else in the long run. Let's be superficial and pity the poor Philosophers. Let's blow trumpets and squeakers, and enjoy the party as much as we can, like very small, quite idiotic school-children. Let's savour the delight of the moment. Come and kiss me, darling, before your body rots, and worms pop in and out of your eye sockets.

Amanda Elyot, worms don't pop.

Elyot (*kissing her*) I don't mind, what you do see? You can paint yourself bright green all over, and dance naked in the Place Vendôme, and rush off madly with all the men in the world, and I shan't say a word, as long as you love me best.

Amanda Thank you, dear. The same applies to you, except that if I catch you so much as looking at another woman, I'll kill you.

Elyot Do you remember that awful scene we had in Venice?

Amanda Which particular one?

Elyot The one when you bought that little painted wooden snake on the Piazza, and put it on my bed.

Amanda Oh Charles. That was his name, Charles. He did wriggle so beautifully.

Elyot Horrible thing, I hated it.

Amanda Yes, I know you did. You threw it out of the window into the Grand Canal. I don't think I'll ever forgive you for that.

Elyot How long did the row last?

Amanda It went on intermittently for days.

Elyot The worst one was in Cannes when your curling

irons burnt a hole in my new dressing-gown. (*He laughs.*)

Amanda   It burnt my comb too, and all the towels in the bathroom.

Elyot   That was a rouser, wasn't it?

Amanda   That was the first time you ever hit me.

Elyot   I didn't hit you very hard.

Amanda   The manager came in and found us rolling on the floor, biting and scratching like panthers. Oh dear, oh dear – (*She laughs helplessly.*)

Elyot   I shall never forget his face. (*They both collapse with laughter.*)

Amanda   How ridiculous, how utterly, utterly ridiculous.

Elyot   We were very much younger then.

Amanda   And very much sillier.

Elyot   As a matter of fact the real cause of that row was Peter Burden.

Amanda   You knew there was nothing in that.

Elyot   I didn't know anything of the sort, you took presents from him.

Amanda   Presents: only a trivial little brooch.

Elyot   I remember it well, bristling with diamonds. In the worst possible taste.

Amanda   Not at all, it was very pretty. I still have it, and I wear it often.

Elyot   You went out of your way to torture me over Peter Burden.

Amanda   No, I didn't, you worked the whole thing up in your jealous imagination.

Elyot   You must admit that he was in love with you, wasn't he?

Amanda Just a little perhaps. Nothing serious.

Elyot You let him kiss you. You said you did.

Amanda Well, what of it?

Elyot What of it!

Amanda It gave him a lot of pleasure, and it didn't hurt me.

Elyot What about me?

Amanda If you hadn't been so suspicious and nosey you'd never have known a thing about it.

Elyot That's a nice point of view I must say.

Amanda Oh dear, I'm bored with this conversation.

Elyot So am I, bored stiff. (*He goes over to the table.*) Want some brandy?

Amanda No thanks.

Elyot I'll have a little, I think.

Amanda I don't see why you want it, you've already had two glasses.

Elyot No particular reason, anyhow they were very small ones.

Amanda It seems so silly to go on, and on, and on with a thing.

Elyot (*pouring himself out a glassful*) You can hardly call three liqueur glasses in a whole evening going on, and on, and on.

Amanda It's become a habit with you.

Elyot You needn't be so grand, just because you don't happen to want any yourself at the moment.

Amanda Don't be so stupid.

Elyot (*irritably*) Really, Amanda –

Amanda   What?

Elyot   Nothing. (**Amanda** *sits down on the sofa, and, taking a small mirror from her bag, gazes at her face critically, and then uses some lipstick and powder. A trifle nastily.*) Going out somewhere dear?

Amanda   No, just making myself fascinating for you.

Elyot   That reply has broken my heart.

Amanda   The woman's job is to allure the man. Watch me a minute, will you?

Elyot   As a matter of fact that's perfectly true.

Amanda   Oh, no, it isn't.

Elyot   Yes it is.

Amanda (*snappily*)   Oh be quiet.

Elyot   It's a pity you didn't have any more brandy; it might have made you a little less disagreeable.

Amanda   It doesn't seem to have worked such wonders with you.

Elyot   Snap, snap, snap; like a little adder.

Amanda   Adders don't snap, they sting.

Elyot   Nonsense, they have a little bag of venom behind their fangs and they snap.

Amanda   They sting.

Elyot   They snap.

Amanda (*with exasperation*)   I don't care, do you understand? I don't care. I don't mind if they bark, and roll about like hoops.

Elyot (*after a slight pause*)   Did you see much of Peter Burden after our divorce?

Amanda   Yes, I did, quite a lot.

Elyot I suppose you let him kiss you a good deal more then.

Amanda Mind your own business.

Elyot You must have had a riotous time. (**Amanda** *doesn't answer, so he stalks about the room.*) No restraint at all – very enjoyable – you never had much anyhow.

Amanda You're quite insufferable; I expect it's because you're drunk.

Elyot I'm not in the least drunk.

Amanda You always had a weak head.

Elyot I think I mentioned once before that I have only had three minute liqueur glasses of brandy the whole evening long. A child of two couldn't get drunk on that.

Amanda On the contrary, a child of two could get violently drunk on only one glass of brandy.

Elyot Very interesting. How about a child of four, and a child of six, and a child of nine?

Amanda (*turning her head away*) Oh do shut up.

Elyot (*witheringly*) We might get up a splendid little debate about that, you know, Intemperate Tots.

Amanda Not very funny, dear; you'd better have some more brandy.

Elyot Very good idea, I will. (*He pours out another glass and gulps it down defiantly.*)

Amanda Ridiculous ass.

Elyot I beg your pardon?

Amanda I said ridiculous ass!

Elyot (*with great dignity*) Thank you. (*There is a silence.* **Amanda** *gets up, and turns the gramophone on.*) You'd better turn that off, I think.

Amanda (*coldly*) Why?

Elyot   It's very late and it will annoy the people upstairs.

Amanda   There aren't any people upstairs. It's a photographer's studio.

Elyot   There are people downstairs, I suppose?

Amanda   They're away in Tunis.

Elyot   This is no time of the year for Tunis. (*He turns the gramophone off.*)

Amanda (*icily*)   Turn it on again, please.

Elyot   I'll do no such thing.

Amanda   Very well, if you insist on being boorish and idiotic. (*She gets up and turns it on again.*)

Elyot   Turn it off. It's driving me mad.

Amanda   You're far too temperamental. Try to control yourself.

Elyot   Turn it off.

Amanda   I won't. (**Elyot** *rushes at the gramophone.* **Amanda** *tries to ward him off. They struggle silently for a moment then the needle screeches across the record.*) There now, you've ruined the record. (*She takes it off and scrutinises it.*)

Elyot   Good job, too.

Amanda   Disagreeable pig.

Elyot (*suddenly stricken with remorse*)   Amanda darling – Sollocks.

Amanda (*furiously*)   Sollocks yourself. (*She breaks the record over his head.*)

Elyot (*staggering*)   You spiteful little beast. (*He slaps her face. She screams loudly and hurls herself sobbing with rage on to the sofa, with her face buried in the cushions.*)

Amanda (*wailing*)   Oh, oh, oh –

Elyot   I'm sorry, I didn't mean it – I'm sorry, darling, I swear I didn't mean it.

Amanda   Go away, go away, I hate you. (**Elyot** *kneels on the sofa and tries to pull her round to look at him.*)

Elyot   Amanda – listen – listen –

Amanda   (*turning suddenly, and fetching him a welt across the face*)   Listen indeed; I'm sick and tired of listening to you, you damned sadistic bully.

Elyot   (*with great grandeur*)   Thank you.

He stalks towards the door, in stately silence. **Amanda** *throws a cushion at him, which misses him and knocks down a lamp and a vase on the side table.*

Elyot   (*laughing falsely*)   A pretty display I must say.

Amanda   (*wildly*)   Stop laughing like that.

Elyot   (*continuing*)   Very amusing indeed.

Amanda   (*losing control*)   Stop – stop – stop – (*She rushes at him, he grabs her hands and they sway about the room, until he manages to twist her round by the arms so that she faces him, closely, quivering with fury.*) – I hate you – do you hear? You're conceited, and overbearing, and utterly impossible!

Elyot   (*shouting her down*)   You're a vile-tempered loose-living wicked little beast, and I never want to see you again so long as I live.

He flings her away from him, she staggers, and falls against a chair. They stand gasping at one another in silence for a moment.

Amanda   (*very quietly*)   This is the end, do you understand? The end, finally and for ever.

She goes to the door, which opens on to the landing, and wrenches it open. He rushes after her and clutches her wrist.

Elyot   You're not going like this.

Amanda   Oh yes I am.

Elyot   You're not.

Amanda   I am; let go of me –

He pulls her away from the door, and once more they struggle. This time a standard lamp crashes to the ground.

Amanda (*breathlessly, as they fight*)   You're a cruel fiend, and I hate and loathe you; thank God I've realised in time what you're really like; marry you again, never, never, never ... I'd rather die in torment –

Elyot (*at the same time*)   Shut up; shut up. I wouldn't marry you again if you came crawling to me on your bended knees, you're a mean, evil-minded, little vampire – I hope to God I never set eyes on you again as long as I live –

At this point in the proceedings they trip over a piece of carpet, and fall on to the floor, rolling over and over in paroxysms of rage.
Victor *and* **Sibyl** *enter quietly, through the open door, and stand staring at them in horror. Finally* **Amanda** *breaks free and half gets up,* **Elyot** *grabs her leg, and she falls against a table, knocking it completely over.*

Amanda (*screaming*)   Beast; brute; swine; cad; beast; beast; brute; devil –

She rushes back at **Elyot**, *who is just rising to his feet, and gives him a stinging blow, which knocks him over again. She rushes blindly off left, and slams the door, at the same moment that he jumps up and rushes off right, also slamming the door.* **Victor** *and* **Sibyl** *advance apprehensively into the room, and sink on to the sofa –*

The curtain falls.

Act Three

The scene is the same as Act Two. It is the next morning. The time is about eight-thirty. **Victor** *and* **Sibyl** *have drawn the two sofas across the doors right, and left, and are stretched on them, asleep.* **Victor** *is in front of* **Amanda**'s *door, and* **Sibyl** *in front of* **Elyot**'s.

The room is in chaos, as it was left the night before.

As the curtain rises, there is the rattling of a key in the lock of the front door, and **Louise** *enters. She is rather a frowsy looking girl, and carries a string bag with various bundles of eatables crammed into it, notably a long roll of bread, and a lettuce. She closes the door after her, and in the half light trips over the standard lamp lying on the floor. She puts her string bag down, and gropes her way over to the window. She draws the curtains, letting sunlight stream into the room. When she looks round, she gives a little cry of horror. Then she sees* **Victor** *and* **Sibyl** *sleeping peacefully, and comes over and scrutinises each of them with care, then she shakes* **Sibyl** *by the shoulder.*

Sibyl (*waking*) Oh dear.

Louise Bon jour, Madame.

Sibyl (*bewildered*) What? – Oh – bon jour.

Louise Qu'est-ce que vous faites ici, Madame?

Sibyl What – what? – Wait a moment, attendez un instant – oh dear –

Victor (*sleepily*) What's happening? (*Jumping up.*) Of course, I remember now. (*He sees* **Louise**.) Oh!

Louise (*firmly*) Bon jour, Monsieur:

Victor Er – bon jour – What time is it?

Louise (*rather dully*) Eh, Monsieur?

Sibyl (*sitting up on the sofa*) Quelle heure est il s'il vous plait?

Louise   C'est neuf heures moins dix, Madame.

Victor   What did she say?

Sibyl   I think she said nearly ten o'clock.

Victor (*taking situation in hand*)   Er – voulez – er – wake – revillez Monsieur et Madame – er toute suite?

Louise (*shaking her head*)   Non, Monsieur. Il m'est absolument defendu de les appeler jusqu'à ce qu'ils sonnent.

She takes her bag and goes off into the kitchen. **Victor** *and* **Sibyl** *look at each other helplessly.*

Sibyl   What are we to do?

Victor (*with determination*)   Wake them ourselves. (*He goes towards* **Amanda**'s *door.*)

Sibyl   No, no, wait a minute.

Victor   What's the matter?

Sibyl (*plaintively*)   I couldn't face them yet, really, I couldn't; I feel dreadful.

Victor   So do I. (*He wanders gloomily over to the window.*) It's a lovely morning.

Sibyl   Lovely. (*She bursts into tears.*)

Victor (*coming to her*)   I say, don't cry.

Sibyl   I can't help it.

Victor   Please don't, please –

Sibyl   It's all so squalid, I wish we hadn't stayed; what's the use?

Victor   We've got to see them before we go back to England, we must get things straightened out.

Sibyl (*sinking down on to the sofa*)   Oh dear, oh dear, oh dear, I wish I were dead.

Victor   Hush, now, hush. Remember your promise. We've

got to see this through together and get it settled one way or another.

Sibyl (*sniffling*) I'll try to control myself, only I'm so . . . so tired, I haven't slept properly for ages.

Victor Neither have I.

Sibyl If we hadn't arrived when we did, they'd have killed one another.

Victor They must have been drunk.

Sibyl She hit him.

Victor He'd probably hit her, too, earlier on.

Sibyl I'd no idea anyone ever behaved like that; it's so disgusting, so degrading, Elli of all people – oh dear – (*She almost breaks down again, but controls herself.*)

Victor What an escape you've had.

Sibyl What an escape we've both had.

Amanda *opens her door and looks out. She is wearing travelling clothes, and is carrying a small suitcase. She jumps, upon seeing* **Sibyl** *and* **Victor**.

Amanda Oh! – good morning.

Victor (*with infinite reproach in his voice*) Oh, Amanda.

Amanda Will you please move this sofa, I can't get out.

Victor *moves the sofa, and she advances into the room and goes towards the door.*

Victor Where are you going?

Amanda Away.

Victor You can't.

Amanda Why not?

Victor I want to talk to you.

Amanda (*wearily*) What on earth is the use of that?

Victor I must talk to you.

Amanda Well, all I can say is, it's very inconsiderate. (*She plumps the bag down by the door and comes down to* **Victor**.)

Victor Mandy, I –

Amanda (*gracefully determined to rise above the situation*) I suppose you're Sibyl; how do you do? (**Sibyl** *turns her back on her.*) Well, if you're going to take up that attitude, I fail to see the point of your coming here at all.

Sibyl I came to see Elyot.

Amanda I've no wish to prevent you, he's in there, probably wallowing in an alcoholic stupor.

Victor This is all very unpleasant, Amanda.

Amanda I quite agree, that's why I want to go away.

Victor That would be shirking; this must be discussed at length.

Amanda Very well, if you insist, but not just now, I don't feel up to it. Has Louise come yet?

Victor If Louise is the maid, she's in the kitchen.

Amanda Thank you. You'd probably like some coffee, excuse me a moment. (*She goes off into the kitchen.*)

Sibyl Well! How dare she?

Victor (*irritably*) How dare she what?

Sibyl Behave so calmly, as though nothing had happened.

Victor I don't see what else she could have done.

Sibyl Insufferable I call it.

Elyot *opens his door and looks out.*

Elyot (*seeing them*) Oh God.

He shuts the door again quickly.

Sibyl Elyot – Elyot – (*She rushes over to the door and bangs on it.*) Elyot – Elyot – Elyot –

Elyot (*inside*)   Go away.

Sibyl (*falling on to the sofa*)   Oh, oh, oh.

She bursts into tears again.

Victor   Do pull yourself together for heaven's sake.

Sibyl   I can't, I can't – oh, oh, oh –

Amanda *re-enters.*

Amanda   I've ordered some coffee and rolls, they'll be here soon. I must apologise for the room being so untidy.

She picks up a cushion, and pats it into place on the sofa. There is a silence except for **Sibyl**'s *sobs.* **Amanda** *looks at her, and then at* **Victor**; *then she goes off into her room again, and shuts the door.*

Victor   It's no use crying like that, it doesn't do any good.

After a moment, during which **Sibyl** *makes renewed efforts to control her tears,* **Elyot** *opens the door immediately behind her, pushes the sofa, with her on it, out of the way, and walks towards the front door. He is in travelling clothes, and carrying a small suitcase.*

Sibyl (*rushing after him*)   Elyot, where are you going?

Elyot   Canada.

Sibyl   You can't go like this, you can't.

Elyot   I see no point in staying.

Victor   You owe it to Sibyl to stay.

Elyot   How do you do, I don't think we've met before.

Sibyl   You must stay, you've got to stay.

Elyot   Very well, if you insist. (*He plumps his bag down.*) I'm afraid the room is in rather a mess. Have you seen the maid Louise?

Victor   She's in the kitchen.

Elyot   Good. I'll order some coffee.

He makes a movement towards the kitchen.

Victor (*stopping him*)   No, your – er – my – er – Amanda has already ordered it.

Elyot   Oh, I'm glad the old girl's up and about.

Victor   We've got to get things straightened out, you know.

Elyot (*looking around the room*)   Yes, it's pretty awful. We'll get the concierge up from downstairs.

Victor   You're being purposely flippant, but it's no good.

Elyot   Sorry. (*He lapses into silence.*)

Victor (*after a pause*)   What's to be done?

Elyot   I don't know.

Sibyl (*with spirit*)   It's all perfectly horrible. I feel smirched and unclean as though slimy things had been crawling all over me.

Elyot   Maybe they have, that's a very old sofa.

Victor   If you don't stop your damned flippancy, I'll knock your head off.

Elyot (*raising his eyebrows*)   Has it ever struck you that flippancy might cover a very real embarrassment?

Victor   In a situation such as this, it's in extremely bad taste.

Elyot   No worse than bluster, and invective. As a matter of fact, as far as I know, this situation is entirely without precedent. We have no prescribed etiquette to fall back upon. I shall continue to be flippant.

Sibyl   Oh, Elyot, how can you – how can you.

Elyot   I'm awfully sorry, Sibyl.

Victor   It's easy enough to be sorry.

Elyot   On the contrary. I find it exceedingly difficult. I seldom regret anything. This is a very rare and notable exception, a sort of red-letter day. We must all make the most of it.

Sibyl   I'll never forgive you, never. I wouldn't have believed anyone could be so callous and cruel.

Elyot   I absolutely see your point, and as I said before, I'm sorry.

There is silence for a moment. Then **Amanda** *comes in again. She has obviously decided to carry everything off in a high-handed manner.*

Amanda (*in social tones*)   What! Breakfast not ready yet? Really, these French servants are too slow for words. (*She smiles gaily.*) What a glorious morning. (*She goes to the window.*) I do love Paris, it's so genuinely gay. Those lovely trees in the Champs Elysées, and the little roundabouts for the children to play on, and those shiny red taxis. You can see Sacre Cœur quite clearly today, sometimes it's a bit misty, particularly in August, all the heat rising up from the pavements, you know.

Elyot (*drily*)   Yes, dear, we know.

Amanda (*ignoring him*)   And it's heavenly being so high up. I found this flat three years ago, quite by merest chance. I happened to be staying at the Plaza Athenee, just down the road –

Elyot (*enthusiastically*)   Such a nice hotel, with the most enchanting courtyard with a fountain that goes plopplopplopplopplopplopplopplopplop –

Victor   This is ridiculous, Amanda.

Elyot (*continuing*)   Plop plop plop plop plop plop plop plop plop plop –

Amanda (*overriding him*)   Now, Victor, I refuse to discuss anything in the least important until after breakfast. I couldn't concentrate now, I know I couldn't.

Elyot (*sarcastically*)   What manner. What poise. How I envy it. To be able to carry off the most embarrassing situation

with such tact, and delicacy, and above all – such subtlety.
Go on, Amanda, you're making everything so much easier.
We shall all be playing Hunt the Slipper in a minute.

Amanda Please don't address me, I don't wish to speak
to you.

Elyot Splendid.

Amanda And what's more, I never shall again as long as
I live.

Elyot I shall endeavour to rise above it.

Amanda I've been brought up to believe that it's beyond
the pale, for a man to strike a woman.

Elyot A very poor tradition. Certain women should be
struck regularly, like gongs.

Amanda You're an unmitigated cad, and a bully.

Elyot And you're an ill-mannered, bad-tempered slattern.

Amanda (*loudly*) Slattern indeed.

Elyot Yes, slattern, slattern, slattern, and fishwife.

Victor Keep your mouth shut, you swine.

Elyot Mind your own damned business.

They are about to fight, when **Sibyl** *rushes between them.*

Sibyl Stop, stop, it's no use going on like this. Stop,
please. (*To* **Amanda**.) Help me, do, do, do, help me –

Amanda I'm not going to interfere. Let them fight if
they want to, it will probably clear the air anyhow.

Sibyl Yes but –

Amanda Come into my room, perhaps you'd like to
wash or something.

Sibyl No, but –

Amanda (*firmly*) Come along.

Sibyl   Very well.

She tosses her head at **Elyot**, *and* **Amanda** *drags her off.*

Victor (*belligerently*)   Now then!

Elyot   Now then what?

Victor   Are you going to take back those things you said to Amanda?

Elyot   Certainly. I'll take back anything, if only you'll stop bellowing at me.

Victor (*contemptuously*)   You're a coward too.

Elyot   They want us to fight, don't you see?

Victor   No, I don't, why should they?

Elyot   Primitive feminine instincts – warring males – very enjoyable.

Victor   You think you're very clever, don't you?

Elyot   I think I'm a bit cleverer than you, but apparently that's not saying much.

Victor (*violently*)   What?

Elyot   Oh, do sit down.

Victor   I will not.

Elyot   Well, if you'll excuse me, I will, I'm extremely tired.

He sits down.

Victor   Oh, for God's sake, behave like a man.

Elyot (*patiently*)   Listen a minute, all this belligerency is very right and proper and highly traditional, but if only you'll think for a moment, you'll see that it won't get us very far.

Victor   To hell with all that.

Elyot   I should like to explain that if you hit me, I shall certainly hit you, probably equally hard, if not harder. I'm just as strong as you I should imagine. Then you'd hit me again, and I'd hit you again, and we'd go on until one or the other was knocked out. Now if you'll explain to me satisfactorily how all that can possibly improve the situation, I'll tear off my coat, and we'll go at one another hammer and tongs, immediately.

Victor It would ease my mind.

Elyot Only if you won.

Victor I should win all right.

Elyot Want to try?

Victor Yes.

Elyot (*jumping up*) Here goes then –

He tears off his coat.

Victor Just a moment.

Elyot Well?

Victor What did you mean about them wanting us to fight?

Elyot It would be balm to their vanity.

Victor Do you love Amanda?

Elyot Is this a battle or a discussion? If it's the latter I shall put on my coat again, I don't want to catch a chill.

Victor Answer my question, please.

Elyot Have a cigarette?

Victor (*stormily*) Answer my question.

Elyot If you analyse it, it's rather a silly question.

Victor Do you love Amanda?

Elyot (*confidentially*) Not very much this morning to be perfectly frank, I'd like to wring her neck. Do you love her?

Victor   That's beside the point.

Elyot   On the contrary, it's the crux of the whole affair. If you do love her still, you can forgive her, and live with her in peace and harmony until you're ninety-eight.

Victor   You're apparently even more of a cad than I thought you were.

Elyot   You are completely in the right over the whole business, don't imagine I'm not perfectly conscious of that.

Victor   I'm glad.

Elyot   It's all very unfortunate.

Victor   Unfortunate: My God!

Elyot   It might have been worse.

Victor   I'm glad you think so.

Elyot   I do wish you'd stop being so glad about everything.

Victor   What do you intend to do? That's what I want to know. What do you intend to do?

Elyot   (*suddenly serious*)   I don't know, I don't care.

Victor   I suppose you realise that you've broken that poor little woman's heart?

Elyot   Which poor little woman?

Victor   Sibyl, of course.

Elyot   Oh, come now, not as bad as that. She'll get over it, and forget all about me.

Victor   I sincerely hope so ... for her sake.

Elyot   Amanda will forget all about me too. Everybody will forget all about me. I might just as well lie down and die in fearful pain and suffering, nobody would care.

Victor   Don't talk such rot.

Elyot   You must forgive me for taking rather a gloomy

view of everything but the fact is, I suddenly feel slightly depressed.

Victor I intend to divorce Amanda, naming you as co-respondent.

Elyot Very well.

Victor And Sibyl will divorce you for Amanda. It would be foolish of either of you to attempt any defence.

Elyot Quite.

Victor And the sooner you marry Amanda again, the better.

Elyot I'm not going to marry Amanda.

Victor What?

Elyot She's a vile-tempered wicked woman.

Victor You should have thought of that before.

Elyot I did think of it before.

Victor (*firmly*) You've got to marry her.

Elyot I'd rather marry a ravening Leopard.

Victor (*angrily*) Now look here. I'm sick of all this shilly-shallying. You're getting off a good deal more lightly than you deserve; you can consider yourself damned lucky I didn't shoot you.

Elyot (*with sudden vehemence*) Well, if you'd had a spark of manliness in you, you would have shot me. You're all fuss and fume, one of these cotton-wool Englishmen. I despise you.

Victor (*through clenched teeth*) You despise me?

Elyot Yes, utterly. You're nothing but a rampaging gas bag!

He goes off into his room and slams the door, leaving **Victor** *speechless with fury.* **Amanda** *and* **Sibyl** *re-enter.*

Amanda (*brightly*) Well, what's happened?

Victor (*sullenly*) Nothing's happened.

Amanda You ought to be ashamed to admit it.

Sibyl Where's Elyot?

Victor In there.

Amanda What's he doing?

Victor (*turning angrily away*) How do I know what he's doing?

Amanda If you were half the man I thought you were, he'd be bandaging himself.

Sibyl (*with defiance*) Elyot's just as strong as Victor.

Amanda (*savagely*) I should like it proved.

Sibyl There's no need to be so vindictive.

Amanda You were abusing Elyot like a pick-pocket to me a little while ago, now you are standing up for him.

Sibyl I'm beginning to suspect that he wasn't quite so much to blame as I thought.

Amanda Oh really?

Sibyl You certainly have a very unpleasant temper.

Amanda It's a little difficult to keep up with your rapid changes of front, but you're young and inexperienced, so I forgive you freely.

Sibyl (*heatedly*) Seeing the depths of degradation to which age and experience have brought you, I'm glad I'm as I am!

Amanda (*with great grandeur*) That was exceedingly rude. I think you'd better go away somewhere. (*She waves her hand vaguely.*)

Sibyl After all, Elyot is my husband.

Amanda Take him with you, by all means.

Sibyl If you're not very careful, I will! (*She goes over to*

Elyot's *door and bangs on it.*) Elyot – Elyot –

Elyot (*inside*)   What is it?

Sibyl   Let me in. Please, please let me in; I want to speak to you!

Amanda   Heaven preserve me from nice women!

Sibyl   Your own reputation ought to do that.

Amanda (*irritably*)   Oh, go to hell!

Elyot *opens the door, and* **Sibyl** *disappears inside,* **Amanda** *looks at* **Victor**, *who is standing with his back turned, staring out of the window, then she wanders about the room, making rather inadequate little attempts to tidy up. She glances at* **Victor** *again.*

Amanda   Victor.

Victor (*without turning*)   What?

Amanda (*sadly*)   Nothing.

She begins to wrestle with one of the sofas in an effort to get it in place. **Victor** *turns, sees her, and comes down and helps her, in silence.*

Victor   Where does it go?

Amanda   Over there. (*After they have placed it,* **Amanda** *sits on the edge of it and gasps a little.*) Thank you, Victor.

Victor   Don't mention it.

Amanda (*after a pause*)   What did you say to Elyot?

Victor   I told him he was beneath contempt.

Amanda   Good.

Victor   I think you must be mad, Amanda.

Amanda   I've often thought that myself.

Victor   I feel completely lost, completely bewildered.

Amanda   I don't blame you. I don't feel any too cosy.

Victor   Had you been drinking last night?

Amanda Certainly not!

Victor Had Elyot been drinking?

Amanda Yes – gallons.

Victor Used he to drink before? When you were married to him?

Amanda Yes, terribly. Night after night he'd come home roaring and hiccoughing.

Victor Disgusting!

Amanda Yes, wasn't it?

Victor Did he really strike you last night?

Amanda Repeatedly. I'm bruised beyond recognition.

Victor (*suspecting slight exaggeration*) Amanda!

Amanda (*putting her hand on his arm*) Oh, Victor, I'm most awfully sorry to have given you so much trouble, really I am! I've behaved badly, I know, but something strange happened to me. I can't explain it, there's no excuse, but I am ashamed of having made you unhappy.

Victor I can't understand it at all. I've tried to, but I can't. It all seems so unlike you.

Amanda It isn't really unlike me, that's the trouble. I ought never to have married you; I'm a bad lot.

Victor Amanda!

Amanda Don't contradict me. I know I'm a bad lot.

Victor I wasn't going to contradict you.

Amanda Victor!

Victor You appal me – absolutely!

Amanda Go on, go on, I deserve it.

Victor I didn't come here to accuse you; there's no sense in that!

Amanda Why did you come?

Victor To find out what you want me to do.

Amanda Divorce me, I suppose, as soon as possible. I won't make any difficulties. I'll go away, far away, Morocco, or Tunis, or somewhere. I shall probably catch some dreadful disease, and die out there, all alone – oh dear!

Victor It's no use pitying yourself.

Amanda I seem to be the only one who does. I might just as well enjoy it. (*She sniffs.*) I'm thoroughly unprincipled; Sibyl was right!

Victor (*irritably*) Sibyl's an ass.

Amanda (*brightening slightly*) Yes, she is rather, isn't she? I can't think why Elyot ever married her.

Victor Do you love him?

Amanda She seems so insipid, somehow –

Victor Do you love him?

Amanda Of course she's very pretty, I suppose, in rather a shallow way, but still –

Victor Amanda!

Amanda Yes, Victor?

Victor You haven't answered my question.

Amanda I've forgotten what it was.

Victor (*turning away*) You're hopeless – hopeless.

Amanda Don't be angry, it's all much too serious to be angry about.

Victor You're talking utter nonsense!

Amanda No, I'm not, I mean it. It's ridiculous for us all to stand round arguing with one another. You'd much better go back to England and let your lawyers deal with the whole thing.

Victor   But what about you?

Amanda   I'll be all right.

Victor   I only want to know one thing, and you won't tell me.

Amanda   What is it?

Victor   Do you love Elyot?

Amanda   No, I hate him. When I saw him again suddenly at Deauville, it was an odd sort of shock. It swept me away completely. He attracted me; he always has attracted me, but only the worst part of me. I see that now.

Victor   I can't understand why? He's so terribly trivial and superficial.

Amanda   That sort of attraction can't be explained, it's a sort of chemical what d'you call 'em.

Victor   Yes; it must be!

Amanda   I don't expect you to understand, and I'm not going to try to excuse myself in any way. Elyot was the first love affair of my life, and in spite of all the suffering he caused me before, there must have been a little spark left smouldering, which burst into flame when I came face to face with him again. I completely lost grip of myself and behaved like a fool, for which I shall pay all right, you needn't worry about that. But perhaps one day, when all this is dead and done with, you and I might meet and be friends. That's something to hope for, anyhow. Goodbye, Victor dear. (*She holds out her hand.*)

Victor   (*shaking her hand mechanically*)   Do you want to marry him?

Amanda   I'd rather marry a boa constrictor.

Victor   I can't go away and leave you with a man who drinks, and knocks you about.

Amanda You needn't worry about leaving me, as though I were a sort of parcel. I can look after myself.

Victor You said just now you were going away to Tunis, to die.

Amanda I've changed my mind, it's the wrong time of the year for Tunis. I shall go somewhere quite different. I believe Brioni is very nice in the summer.

Victor Why won't you be serious for just one moment?

Amanda I've told you, it's no use.

Victor If it will make things any easier for you, I won't divorce you.

Amanda Victor!

Victor We can live apart until Sibyl has got her decree against Elyot, then, some time after that, I'll let you divorce me.

Amanda (*turning away*) I see you're determined to make me serious, whether I like it or not.

Victor I married you because I loved you.

Amanda Stop it, Victor! Stop it! I won't listen!

Victor I expect I love you still; one doesn't change all in a minute. You never loved me. I see that now, of course, so perhaps everything has turned out for the best really.

Amanda I thought I loved you, honestly I did.

Victor Yes, I know, that's all right.

Amanda What an escape you've had.

Victor I've said that to myself often during the last few days.

Amanda There's no need to rub it in.

Victor Do you agree about the divorce business?

Amanda Yes. It's very, very generous of you.

Victor It will save you some of the mud-slinging. We might persuade Sibyl not to name you.

Amanda (*ruefully*) Yes, we might.

Victor Perhaps she'll change her mind about divorcing him.

Amanda Perhaps. She certainly went into the bedroom with a predatory look in her eye.

Victor Would you be pleased if that happened?

Amanda Delighted.

She laughs suddenly. **Victor** *looks at her, curiously.* **Sibyl** *and* **Elyot** *come out of the bedroom. There is an awkward silence for a moment.*

Sibyl (*looking at* **Amanda** *triumphantly*) Elyot and I have come to a decision.

Amanda How very nice!

Victor What is it?

Amanda Don't be silly, Victor. Look at their faces.

Elyot Feminine intuition, very difficult.

Amanda (*looking at* **Sibyl**) Feminine determination, very praiseworthy.

Sibyl I am not going to divorce Elyot for a year.

Amanda I congratulate you.

Elyot (*defiantly*) Sibyl has behaved like an angel.

Amanda Well, it was certainly her big moment.

Louise *comes staggering in with a large tray of coffee and rolls, etc., she stands peering over the edge of it, not knowing where to put it.*

Elyot Il faut le met sur la petite table la bas.

Louise Oui, Monsieur.

Elyot *and* **Victor** *hurriedly clear the things off the side table, and* **Louise** *puts the tray down, and goes back into the kitchen.* **Amanda** *and* **Sibyl** *eye one another.*

Amanda It all seems very amicable.

Sibyl It is, thank you.

Amanda I don't wish to depress you, but Victor isn't going to divorce me either.

Elyot (*looking up sharply*) What!

Amanda I believe I asked you once before this morning, never to speak to me again.

Elyot I only said 'What'. It was a general exclamation denoting extreme satisfaction.

Amanda (*politely to* **Sibyl**) Do sit down, won't you?

Sibyl I'm afraid I must be going now. I'm catching the Golden Arrow; it leaves at twelve.

Elyot (*coaxingly*) You have time for a little coffee surely?

Sibyl No, I really must go!

Elyot I shan't be seeing you again for such a long time.

Amanda (*brightly*) Living apart? How wise!

Elyot (*ignoring her*) Please, Sibyl, do stay!

Sibyl (*looking at* **Amanda** *with a glint in her eye*) Very well, just for a little.

Amanda Sit down, Victor, darling.

They all sit down in silence. **Amanda** *smiles sweetly at* **Sibyl** *and holds up the coffee pot and milk jug.*

Half and half?

Sibyl Yes, please.

Amanda (*sociably*) What would one do without one's morning coffee? That's what I often ask myself.

Elyot   Is it?

Amanda (*withering him with a look*)   Victor, sugar for Sibyl. (*To* **Sibyl**.) It would be absurd for me to call you anything but Sibyl, wouldn't it?

Sibyl (*not to be outdone*)   Of course, I shall call you Mandy.

Amanda *represses a shudder.*

Elyot   Oh God! We're off again. What weather!

Amanda *hands* **Sibyl** *her coffee.*

Sibyl   Thank you.

Victor   What's the time?

Elyot   If the clock's still going after last night, it's ten-fifteen.

Amanda (*handing* **Victor** *cup of coffee*)   Here, Victor dear.

Victor   Thanks.

Amanda   Sibyl, sugar for Victor.

Elyot   I should like some coffee, please.

Amanda *pours some out for him, and hands it to him in silence.*

Amanda (*to* **Victor**)   Brioche?

Victor (*jumping*)   What?

Amanda   Would you like a Brioche?

Victor   No, thank you.

Elyot   I would. And some butter, and some jam. (*He helps himself.*)

Amanda (*to* **Sibyl**)   Have you ever been to Brioni?

Sibyl   No. It's in the Adriatic, isn't it?

Victor   The Baltic, I think.

Sibyl   I made sure it was in the Adriatic.

Amanda   I had an aunt who went there once.

Elyot (*with his mouth full*)   I once had an aunt who went to Tasmania.

Amanda *looks at him stonily. He winks at her, and she looks away hurriedly.*

Victor   Funny how the South of France has become so fashionable in the summer, isn't it?

Sibyl   Yes, awfully funny.

Elyot   I've been laughing about it for months.

Amanda   Personally, I think it's a bit too hot, although of course one can lie in the water all day.

Sibyl   Yes, the bathing is really divine!

Victor   A friend of mine has a house right on the edge of Cape Ferrat.

Sibyl   Really?

Victor   Yes, right on the edge.

Amanda   That must be marvellous!

Victor   Yes, he seems to like it very much.

The conversation languishes slightly.

Amanda (*with great vivacity*)   Do you know, I really think I love travelling more than anything else in the world! It always gives me such a tremendous feeling of adventure. First of all, the excitement of packing, and getting your passport visa'd and everything, then the thrill of actually starting, and trundling along on trains and ships, and then the most thrilling thing of all, arriving at strange places, and seeing strange people, and eating strange foods –

Elyot   And making strange noises afterwards.

Amanda *chokes violently.* **Victor** *jumps up and tries to offer assistance, but she waves him away, and continues to choke.*

Victor (*to* **Elyot**)   That was a damned fool thing to do.

Elyot   How did I know she was going to choke?

Victor (*to* **Amanda**)   Here, drink some coffee.

Amanda (*breathlessly gasping*)   Leave me alone. I'll be all right in a minute.

Victor (*to* **Elyot**)   You waste too much time trying to be funny.

Sibyl (*up in arms*)   It's no use talking to Elyot like that; it wasn't his fault.

Victor   Of course it was his fault entirely, making rotten stupid jokes –

Sibyl   I thought what Elyot said was funny.

Victor   Well, all I can say is, you must have a very warped sense of humour.

Sibyl   That's better than having none at all.

Victor   I fail to see what humour there is in incessant trivial flippancy.

Sibyl   You couldn't be flippant if you tried until you were blue in the face.

Victor   I shouldn't dream of trying.

Sibyl   It must be very sad not to be able to see any fun in anything.

Amanda *stops choking, and looks at* **Elyot**. *He winks at her again, and she smiles.*

Victor   Fun! I should like you to tell me what fun there is in –

Sibyl   I pity you, I really do. I've been pitying you ever since we left Deauville.

Victor   I'm sure it's very nice of you, but quite unnecessary.

Sibyl   And I pity you more than ever now.

Victor   *Why* now particularly?

Sibyl If you don't see why, I'm certainly not going to tell you.

Victor I see no reason for you to try to pick a quarrel with me. I've tried my best to be pleasant to you, and comfort you.

Sibyl You weren't very comforting when I lost my trunk.

Victor I have little patience with people who go about losing luggage.

Sibyl I don't go about losing luggage. It's the first time I've lost anything in my life.

Victor I find that hard to believe.

Sibyl Anyhow, if you'd tipped the porter enough, everything would have been all right. Small economies never pay; it's absolutely no use –

Victor Oh, for God's sake be quiet!

Amanda *lifts her hand as though she were going to interfere, but* **Elyot** *grabs her wrist. They look at each other for a moment, she lets her hand rest in his.*

Sibyl (*rising from the table*) How dare you speak to me like that!

Victor (*also rising*) Because you've been irritating me for days.

Sibyl (*outraged*) Oh!

Victor (*coming down to her*) You're one of the most completely idiotic women I've ever met.

Sibyl And you're certainly the rudest man I've ever met!

Victor Well then, we're quits, aren't we?

Sibyl (*shrilly*) One thing, you'll get your deserts all right.

Victor What do you mean by that?

Sibyl You know perfectly well what I mean. And it'll serve you right for being weak-minded enough to allow that woman to get round you so easily.

Victor What about you? Letting that unprincipled roué persuade you to take him back again!

Amanda *and* **Elyot** *are laughing silently.* **Elyot** *blows her a lingering kiss across the table.*

Sibyl He's nothing of the sort, he's just been victimised, as you were victimised.

Victor Victimised! What damned nonsense!

Sibyl (*furiously*) It isn't damned nonsense! You're very fond of swearing and blustering and threatening, but when it comes to the point you're as weak as water. Why, a blind cat could see what you've let yourself in for.

Victor (*equally furious*) Stop making those insinuations.

Sibyl I'm not insinuating anything. When I think of all the things you said about her, it makes me laugh, it does really; to see how completely she's got you again.

Victor You can obviously speak with great authority, having had the intelligence to marry a drunkard.

Sibyl So that's what she's been telling you. I might have known it! I suppose she said he struck her too!

Victor Yes, she did, and I'm quite sure it's perfectly true.

Sibyl I expect she omitted to tell you that she drank fourteen glasses of brandy last night straight off; and that the reason their first marriage was broken up was that she used to come home at all hours of the night, screaming and hiccoughing.

Victor If he told you that, he's a filthy liar.

Sibyl He isn't – he isn't!

Victor And if you believe it, you're a silly scatter-brained little fool.

Sibyl (*screaming*) How dare you speak to me like that! How dare you! I've never been so insulted in my life! How dare you!

Amanda *and* **Elyot** *rise quietly, and go, hand in hand, towards the front door.*

Victor (*completely giving way*) It's a tremendous relief to me to have an excuse to insult you. I've had to listen to your weeping and wailing for days. You've clacked at me, and snivelled at me until you've nearly driven me insane, and I controlled my nerves and continued to try to help you and look after you, because I was sorry for you. I always thought you were stupid from the first, but I must say I never realised that you were a malicious little vixen as well!

Sibyl (*shrieking*) Stop it! Stop it! You insufferable great brute!

She slaps his face hard, and he takes her by the shoulders and shakes her like a rat, as **Amanda** *and* **Elyot** *go smilingly out of the door, with their suitcases, and —*

The curtain falls.